P9-EKH-203

STARS BETWEEN THE SUN AND MOON

STARS *between*
the SUN *and* MOON

ONE WOMAN'S LIFE IN NORTH KOREA

AND ESCAPE TO FREEDOM

LUCIA JANG *and* **SUSAN McCLELLAND**

with an afterword by Stephan Haggard

Douglas & McIntyre

Douglas and McIntyre (2013) Ltd.
P.O. Box 219, Madeira Park, BC, V0N 2H0
www.douglas-mcintyre.com

Jacket photograph by Tom Tkach
Edited by Barbara Pulling
Jacket design by Anna Comfort O'Keeffe & Carleton Wilson
Text design by Carleton Wilson
Printed and bound in Canada

**Canada Council
for the Arts** **Conseil des Arts
du Canada**

**BRITISH COLUMBIA
ARTS COUNCIL**
An agency of the Province of British Columbia

Douglas and McIntyre (2013) Ltd. acknowledges financial support from the
Government of Canada through the Canada Book Fund and the Canada Council
for the Arts, and from the Province of British Columbia through the BC Arts
Council and the Book Publishing Tax Credit.

Cataloguing information available from Library and Archives Canada
ISBN 978-1-77162-035-2 (cloth)
ISBN 978-1-77162-036-9 (ebook)

* * *

Some names, dates and place names in this account have been changed to protect
those still living in North Korea—also known as Chosun—who could possibly be
imprisoned, tortured or killed for being connected to Lucia Jang. The author refers
to herself as Sunhwa in the pages that follow; Lucia Jang is the name she chose for
herself while living in Canada.

For my three sons, so that they may understand their history and their mother's love for them.

For Soohyun Nam, who sat between Susan McClelland and me nearly every Saturday morning for a year, to translate my story.

And finally, for the numerous, nameless North Koreans who attempted to escape freedom and life, and perished on their journey before they could reach their destination, each with a story filled with as much heartache and pain as well as hope and love as my own.

—Lucia Jang

Table of Contents

Prologue

DEAR TAEBUM,

I am looking at you now, as you sleep in the crib in Ulaanbaatar, Mongolia. My eyes are trained on your stomach as you inhale and exhale. I have never prayed before, but now I feel compelled to do so. I raise my hands the way I saw a South Korean man do in China, a man who wore a cross around his neck and whose home smelled of lavender incense and melting candle wax. I close my eyes, then stop before I can say a single word. You've made a strange sound. I fix the thin sheet around your weak and tired body, and then relax. Your face is calm again.

Taebum, there is so much I want to tell you. You are only a few months old, and I want you to grow wise so that these memories I have decided to place in a diary reach you. I want you to understand the forces that nearly destroyed us, and the force that I now know has kept us alive: love. You were never supposed to live. From the moment you were conceived, no one wanted you: your father, his family, China, the country where you were conceived or Chosun, the country where you were born. There was a forest of people trying to prevent your coming into this world. Even my mother, my *umma*, wanted me to be rid of you.

9

Back before you knew life, when I was in the prison camp and I knew the Party would force me to abort the child I was carrying, I began to sing a song. A light snow had begun to fall, but when I stood close to the window in my cell, I saw sun on a cloudless day. Through the chill that had consumed my body since I fled Chosun, I felt heat. I closed my eyes. "*Jjanghago haeddulnal Doraondanda,*" I sang softly. "A bright sunny day is to come back."

I sang another song in my mind when I lifted you above my head in that plastic bag Abuji, my father, had made for you: the song of the Flower Girl, from the film I had loved so much in my youth. The bag protected you from the cold water and concealed you from the border guards who would have shot us both if they had seen. Only your face was visible, so you could breathe. I carried you across the Tumen River to China. I carried you in my arms here to Mongolia.

I have no idea what life will bring you, my son. We are about to be sent to South Korea, where we will be given an apartment and a new, safe existence. When you are older, I want you to read these words, even though they reveal many things about your mother. I will not hide the truth from you. In the midst of all that I endured I saw the sun, I felt its warmth. You will likely never set foot on the soil of your homeland. Nevertheless, I want you to understand the Chosun that is your soul.

Part One

Chapter One

MY MOTHER RARELY smiled. But when she did, her head would tilt to one side, her crimson-coloured lips parted slightly and her black pupils danced against the pearls of her eyes.

One time when this happened, we were sitting in our front yard, overlooking the crops of corn, beans and potatoes near our home in the small city of Yuseon.

"Daughter," she whispered, pulling me into her arms. The smell of her body mixed with the chamomile scent from the *deulgukhwa* that had bloomed early and through which we had been walking. It was my fourth birthday, on the fifth day of the fifth month. As was customary, I had had a bowl of white rice for my morning meal to celebrate.

My mother stroked her belly, which was swollen. Her second child was due, she had told me, in the tenth month of this year.

"I am all yours for a little while longer, then you will have to share me," she said. Her eyelashes reminded me of the wings of the tiger butterflies I saw in the mornings as they floated around the azaleas in the garden. "I want to tell you many things," she continued. "I just don't know where to begin."

"Umma, I want to know what 'I love you' means." I smiled, relaxing into her arms, feeling her hard stomach against my back. "I heard Abuji say this to you once."

"Hmm. I will tell you. But before I begin, I beg you not to tell others," she said quietly.

"I promise," I said, my gaze falling on some sparrows nearby.

I can't remember all of what my mother said next, Taebum, since I was only a small child at the time. But she told me many stories from my childhood years later and as I grew older, and I will recount some of them for you here.

"MY FAMILY, YOUR ancestors, come from a northern province in Chosun," my mother began. "I grew up in a small cement house with my two sisters and three brothers. I was the eldest. I was the bravest. I was . . . " her words trailed off for a moment. "The most outgoing. I danced my way to school. I sang songs not only about our great father and eternal president, Kim Il-sung, but about flowers and clouds, smiling children. Of course I sang songs from the Soviet Union, too. We all did."

She smiled. "The darkness comes over the garden," she sang for me in her perfect soprano voice. "Even the light has gone to sleep. The night in the suburbs that I love. The nights in the suburbs of Moscow." I loved to sit with my mother and listen to her in this way.

"By the time I was twenty," she continued, "I was a much sought after bride in the city of Hoeryong, where we lived. Men from all over Chosun came to Hoeryong to find their wives because Kim Il-sung's first wife, Lady Kim Jeong-suk, was from there."

"Like Abuji!" I said eagerly. I knew my father had been born in Yuseon. "He went all the way there to find you!"

"Yes," my mother hissed softly, like I imagined one of the tiny green snakes I'd seen in the hills might do. "But there was another man before your father. A military man. With a straighter back than mine and thick shoulders. He was so handsome in his uniform, but he left me with a sinking feeling. I knew we would always remain apart."

"Umma, what is the matter?" I asked, seeing the sadness in my mother's face.

She ignored my question. "I was always called a pretty girl. I had many friends and I loved to sing, but I was never interested in boys. I sang and played the flute at the community centre. After one of my performances, a military man came backstage and said his friend wanted to meet me.

"The year was 1960. I met that military man, and he and his friend and I continued to meet every night following my performances for many months. The man told me I sang like a nightingale. After some time, I knew the day was approaching when he would ask his family if he could marry me. I also knew that before they could say yes, I would have to submit to them a full list of my relatives to show that I came from a patriotic family. A good man, like this man, could only marry a woman loyal to the regime. But I would never be that woman, Sunhwa. I had family members, an uncle and my grandfather, who had fled to the south by ship at the end of the war. My grandfather had helped some American army men who came to the north in search of communists. After the war, the regime started killing anyone who sympathized with the Americans, the enemy. My uncle and grandfather went south to save themselves."

Having a relative leave Chosun for South Korea was the worst thing that could befall a family, she explained seeing my puzzled look.

"I learned this the day I decided to join the political Party and become a *dangwon*. I believed that would show the military man that I was dedicated to the regime and ready to marry him.

That day, I put on my best white *jeogori* along with a black *chima* and *pyunlihwas*, and powdered my face. I planned to meet the military man that night after my performance and tell him what I had done.

"On my way out the door, my father stopped me. 'Ah, Hyesoon,' he moaned. 'Sit down.' He waved to the floor beside the table, where his morning rice was still steaming in a bowl. 'We need to talk.'

"He sat facing me, wringing his hands. His forehead was perspiring, I noticed, despite it being cold inside our home. I was impatient, my fingers tapping my knees.

'You cannot become a Party member, a *dangwon*,' he said stiffly.

"In that moment, hearing his words, I felt as if I had been thrown a thousand *li* backwards.

"'You have relatives in the south,' my father said, hanging his head. 'The Party won't let you join. Why do you think we live here, in a house with no heat, so far from the capital, sharing two rooms among all of us? It's all because your uncle and grandfather fled and are no longer here.'"

My mother sighed, looking off into the distance. "I understood then that only a man who also had a relative disloyal to the regime would take me as a wife. This military man would never be my husband. In this land, where snows blanket the earth for five months a year, choosing a husband for love was a gift that would never warm me."

My mother stopped suddenly. She clasped my hand and pulled me to my feet. We stood watching my father walk up the road toward us in his dark cotton shirt, buttoned at the collar, and matching pants, the same outfit my mother and all our adult neighbours wore. His big black boots made his legs appear heavier than they really were. As he drew near, I could

16

see that his cheeks were red from the wind. His coarse hair was tangled, as if a bird had used it for a nest.

"Remember, what I have told you is our secret," my mother said as she brushed off grass stuck to my navy-blue cotton pants.

"I want to know the ending, Umma," I begged.

"Later. Now we must go. Your grandmother is visiting. She may have brought some extra rice with her."

"CHANGWOON, UH WATNYA?—Are you here?" my grandmother called out, hearing the door open to our house.

I was stopped in the hallway by her cool stare as she and my grandfather approached. My father stepped up beside me.

"Abuji, nae wassugguma," he said. "Father, I am here." This is how we greeted people in Chosun.

I looked into my grandmother's well-lined face. Her lips were so tiny that whenever she wore lipstick, part of the paint bled onto her yellowing skin. "Can I have a candy?" I blurted.

My grandmother reached into her canvas bag, passed my mother a head of cabbage and some white rice, then held her empty hands out in front of her. "I don't have any," she said.

My father's sister and her family lived nearby and now, as I peered around my grandmother and grandfather, I could see my cousin Heeok. Heeok had big brown eyes and a square body that made her look like a cement block. Like me, like all the children we knew, her hair was cut short by her mother, who trimmed it each month with heavy iron scissors.

Heeok's eyes grew large when she spotted me, and she made a show of chewing. She had a candy. I could see it when she opened her mouth.

"But what about her? What is she eating?" I asked my grandmother, defiantly pointing at Heeok.

"I only had one candy, and we visited her first," my grandmother said. I looked pleadingly into Heeok's eyes as she stepped up beside me.

"Why do you always get things I don't?" I whispered.

She just smirked.

That afternoon, for our main meal of the day, we had a few extra spoonfuls of rice with our kimchi. I shovelled the food into my mouth, not stopping until my bowl was empty. I knew my behaviour was not polite and my father might hit me with the broom as later punishment for being rude to visitors. But I was starving. My stomach grumbled even in its sleep. Often, on the day my mother brought home our sparse government rations of white rice, mixed brown rice and other grains, sugar, noodles, and vegetables, I would sit on the floor and devour the noodles uncooked. My mother would squint her eyes, pucker up her lips and shake her head, meaning I was in trouble. She assumed that expression now.

When we were finished our meal, my grandmother announced that her youngest daughter, my father's sister, Youngrahn, would be arriving at our home the next day. "She will stay for a few months, to help you until the baby is born," my grandmother told my mother sternly.

My mother's shoulders slumped, and her eyelids drooped. "I am honoured that Youngrahn will stay here," she replied. It was the polite response, but I knew she was not happy. Even at my young age I has seen on earlier visits Youngrahn was spoiled and demanding.

YOUNGRAHN BREEZED INTO our house the next morning. She threw her coat on the floor in the room where my parents and I slept on cotton mats. "When I start university in a few months, I will get lots of food. The government knows I will need more food then to help me think," she boasted to my mother and me.

"Speaking of food, I'm hungry now."

My mother hung my aunt's coat on a hook on the wall, then headed outside. I heard the creak of the wooden lid that covered the hole in the ground where we stored goat's milk and vegetables. When my mother returned, she began preparing some porridge.

My aunt dug a small mirror from her black leather purse and started to apply cream and pink powder to her face.

"Can I do that too?" I asked, placing one of my hands on her shoulder. She flinched and pushed me away.

"No," she snapped. "This is for grown-ups. But I'll tell you a secret," she said, lowering her voice so my mother wouldn't hear. "Your mother was the most beautiful woman anyone had ever seen when she was young. You might be beautiful too, when you get older."

My body warmed at the thought.

"I'm going out to the movies tonight," my aunt continued. "Maybe I'll meet my future husband there." Her voice grew harsh again. "But no matter how beautiful you become, you will only be eligible for the men women like me reject."

I turned away, my face hot, my palms perspiring, as my mother placed bowls of porridge in front of us.

My mother ate slowly. I followed my auntie's lead and cleared my bowl in a few spoonfuls. My stomach wanted more. I glanced pleadingly at my mother, trying to imagine what she had looked like when she was younger, her face round and soft, her eyebrows perfectly arched. I lifted my spoon and placed it in my mother's bowl.

"You naughty child," my auntie snapped, grabbing my hand and tossing it roughly to the side. "Little one has a gigantic stomach! You are only allowed three hundred grams of food a day. You eat so much. You are a *pig*!"

"It's fine," my mother said calmly, pushing her half-empty bowl toward me.

THAT AFTERNOON, MY mother and I left my auntie alone in the house to nap. We headed to the hills, looking for cabbage or potatoes left behind on the farms following last year's harvest.

"Umma," I said, when we sat down to nibble on some weeds, which on that day were all that we could find. "Can you finish your story? What happened when you told the military man about your uncle and grandfather?"

She sighed. "I didn't tell him at first. He asked me to marry him, and I agreed. I don't know what got into me. I was living in some dream. When he finally announced that his family need-ed the names of all my relatives, I stopped performing. When he came in search of me, I refused to meet him ever again."

"Did you ever see him again, Umma?"

"I did," she said, twirling a strand of hair in her long fingers. "It was after I had moved here with your father. I was walking you in the pram, with your grandmother and auntie. We bumped into the military man on the sidewalk. I was so shocked, I let go of the pram and ran away in a panic.

"When he caught up to me, he was crying. 'Why did you leave me?' he sobbed.

"'Because I have an uncle and grandfather who defected to the south,' I told him, looking around first to make sure your father's mother and sister were nowhere in sight. As you know, it's not right for a married woman ever to speak alone to an un-related man.

"'I don't care about that,' he said, his eyes locked on my own. 'If only you had told me.'

"I didn't know what to say. All my breath had left me. 'You are in the military,' I eventually said. 'How could you hold such a position and be married to me?'

"'I would have left the military to be with you,' he replied. 'I know you have a child now but run away with me. Both of you.'"

My mother turned to face me. "I thought of you, Sunhwa. I thought of the moment when I first felt you stir inside me. I thought of your tiny fingers and how they curled around my own when I held you at night as we slept side by side. I thought of your soft hair and sweet, sticky smell. Then I thought of your father, who had married me despite my past.

"'I have a little girl,' I told the man. 'I am happy with my life now. I don't want to change it. Goodbye.' Then I ran back to find you."

My mother was crying quietly now, her tears dampening my hair. "'I love you' means many things," she said. "It is like that sparrow." She pointed to a tiny bird flying across the path of the setting sun into the pine trees. "If love comes to us, we must let it land. But we must also be prepared to let it go."

Chapter Two

YOUNGRAHN WAS SENT to help my mother because my father had recently been transferred to a factory in Suhdoosoo, a small village in the mountains. He came home every few weeks to check on my mother. As she neared the end of her pregnancy, she was suffering from cramps in her legs. She napped several times a day. Youngrahn didn't prepare meals or sweep the kitchen floor after we ate, however. She spent all her time applying powder and lipstick, going to the cinema and eating our food. While my mother grew larger around the middle, the rest of her body got thinner. The baby hung in her stomach like a big ball. Youngrahn, on the other hand, grew rounder in her face, belly and legs. "Your father is my oldest brother," she said to me when I asked for a spoonful of her noodles. "What is his is mine."

My mother did the laundry in big metal pots in the backyard. I was too little to do more than watch as she lugged the wet cotton blankets to the clothesline and threw them over it. She grimaced from the exertion.

My auntie Youngrahn looked on as my mother stood me naked in the kitchen, except for an undershirt and my panties and washed my shivering body with cool water from the well, scrubbing my hair with our white laundry soap. Whenever

Youngrahn mentioned food, my mother would stop what she was doing and cook white rice or porridge. Umma seldom talked to me now except to issue orders, and she never sang anymore.

On a cool day in the tenth month, as the clouds whistled across the ice-blue sky, my auntie announced she was leaving. By then, I was wearing all three pairs of my pants and all four of my shirts to keep warm while I played in the leaves outside. My aunt packed up all the white rice in our cupboards, as well as her nail file, white face powder, *chima* and hair curlers. She wrapped them in some *bojagi* fabric and then tied it all together into a bundle, the traditional Korean *bottari*.

WITH THE FIRST layer of snow covering the ground and the trees standing bare against the howling wind, my mother woke from her sleep screaming. The sky was still black. I threw off my covers, ran to the window and placed a wooden board over the glass, thinking that the chill seeping in had caused my mother's night terrors.

My mother screamed even more loudly, though, and I knew she was in labour. She had shown me on several occasions what I was to do when this time came. Now I went into action. I dug out the sheets and towels she had washed and folded, then threw on my coat and boots to fetch some wood from the shed. I piled the wood in the stove in the kitchen, just the way my mother had shown me: twigs and pinecones on the bottom, thicker pieces of wood over that and more twigs on top. I stepped back and lit the bottom layer with a long match.

Each time my mother and I had rehearsed this, we would stand watching the flames as they rose and enjoy the feeling as the warm air began to move through the stovepipes underneath the kitchen floor. Tonight, though, I went back out into the dark to get the *ajummas,* married women, the wind slapping my cheeks raw. These women would help my mother bring her baby into the world.

In the early hours of the morning, the house finally became quiet. One of the married women told me my sister had arrived. I stepped gingerly toward the baby, hands over my eyes, afraid to see what the screaming had produced.

I peeked through my fingers to see the tousled black hair of the baby, who was swaddled in a white sheet and suckling at my mother's breast. My father had chosen the name Sunyoung if it was a girl. My mother's face was wet and swollen. Her hair was wet, too. The sheets around her were stained with blood. But when she looked over at me, smiling, her eyes shone like a full moon over the snowy corn fields in midwinter.

One of the married women said next that my mother need- ed to eat and asked me to fetch some food. My mother groaned and said there was not even a grain of rice in the house. The married women sighed to one another, showing their dismay.

MY MOTHER TOLD me that when the baby was a few months old, we would all move to the mountains to be closer to my father's work. My mother said I would like living in Suhdoosoo. The air there was so clean, she told me, that my lungs would feel as if they had been washed with cool water from the well. The mountains would be covered with thick snow in the win- ter, perfect for tobogganing, and with *jindalae* blooms in the springtime.

"You know," my mother said, bending down low so our eyes were level, "your name means first flower. You were born in the fifth month and at the beginning of that month, the *jindalae* be- gins to blossom. By the middle of the month, it is at its fullest. *Jindalae* paves the way for all the other flowers to come."

My sister's presence in the house promised friendship. It promised someone who would remain close, unlike my cousins, who were smug about getting all of my grandmother's pampering. At night, my mother slept with little Sunyoung on one side and me on the other, her green and white duvet covering us.

I liked the way my sister's tiny fingers curled around mine. I lay beside her during the day as my mother packed our belongings into wooden crates.

I would sing a lullaby that my mother had once sung to me. "Sleepy, sleepy, my baby, sleeping well, my baby. Dogs, don't bark! And don't cry, roosters! *Jajang, jajang, oori aga, jaldo janda, oori aga, muhng muhng gae-ya, jitji mara, ggo ggo dakdo, oolij mara.*"

Sometimes my mother joined in. I was happy that song had returned to our home once again.

My grandparents came with us to the train station the day we were scheduled to leave. Summoning my courage, I boldly asked my grandmother: "Why do you get so many candies but never give one to me?"

She folded her arms angrily across her heavy chest. "We have a relative, a son-in-law, who works in the mine. He breathes in lots of metal dust, so he is given the candies and sometimes finger cookies, as *youngyangjeh*—vitamins." My grandmother clicked her tongue. "Won't you learn? These are not the things for you to ask."

I felt my face burn as I took a step backwards. I need vitamins too, I protested silently. And why did my cousin get candies when I didn't. Accidently, one of my heels landed on my grandfather's toes.

"Watch where you are going next time." He spoke in a slow, expressionless voice that made me feel cold, even on a hot, sticky day. I looked away as his tiny eyes bored into me. But as I began to move away from my grandfather, he grabbed my arm, pinching the flesh underneath with his strong fingers, then leaned in close.

"Take this," he whispered, placing something in the pocket of my navy-blue wool coat. His face was so close to mine that I could smell cigarettes on his breath. "Don't tell anyone," he said, letting go of my arm and patting me on the head. "It's our little secret and it's the only one I'll ever give you."

I nodded nervously.

I reached inside my pocket and wrapped my fingers around two hard rectangular objects. My eyes lit up. It was candy.

AT THE STATION in Suhdoosoo, my father met us with another man. The man was much older than my father, and his big head and crooked bowlegs made him look like a frog. The man collected our things and piled them into a box-shaped automobile with a smoke stack on top. It was a "gasoline car," the man explained. He drove the four of us to our new home, a long and narrow cement house attached like a train compartment to a row of similar dwellings. The houses had been built for workers at the power generator station where my father was an engineer helping to design a tunnel system.

My mother set to work instantly, building a fire with wood she found in our new shed. I helped as best I could, unpacking pots and pans, but my attention wandered. Out the window, I could see the winter sun setting behind the snowy mountains. In the fenced-in yard next door, I spied a circular contraption. "A *baeguneh*!" I exclaimed at the sight of the merry-go-round. The wind was shaking it ever so slightly back and forth.

As I watched, some children tumbled out of a large black door into the fenced-in area. They climbed aboard and hung onto the silver bars on top. One boy ran alongside, pulling on the bars to make the whole thing turn. The children spun so fast that their navy-blue hats flew off. Their laughter made me eager to join them.

"If I can go to school," I told my mother that night as I ate my rice and she nursed Sunyoung, "I'm going to like this place a lot."

BUT AS THE days passed, I found myself more alone than ever. The weather was too cold for us to go for walks, and my mother was busy with the baby. Whenever my sister slept, so did my mother. There was no talk of my going to school. I had an eye infection and had to be quarantined at home until I was better. I was left to gaze at the garden next door through the cracks in the ice-glazed window.

Before I knew it, I was celebrating my fifth birthday. It was much like my fourth, with a bowl of white rice for my morning meal. My mother tied my sister onto her back with a piece of fabric, and the three of us went walking in the mountains amidst the fragrant *jindalae*. I found a piece of string just as my feet hit the cement road to our house on the way home. For the next month, that string would be my one and only toy. I wound it around my fingers, twisting it into all sorts of shapes, including snowflakes and goats, until it finally broke.

I dreamed of three things: my sister being old enough to play with me, going to school and riding on the circular contraption and my mother's periodic returns from the food ration centre with the next fortnight's worth of food. Whenever she brought the rations, my sister and I feasted on the raw noodles right on the kitchen floor.

Sadly, my sister was not growing up fast enough, and my eye was not getting better and the food rations were never quite enough. I did find some unexpected playmates: lice. The little bugs nestled in my sister's soft, fine hair. Placing her between my legs, I used a small stick to remove them. It passed the time until my sister got bored, climbed up on her chubby legs and wobbled over to the cupboards where she always found pot lids to bang together.

Sometimes my mother would sneak up behind me while my sister was playing. She'd slide me in between her legs and remove the lice from my head. "I want to tell you a story," she said one winter day as we sat together. It was our second year in the mountains. I settled in eagerly to listen.

"There once was a brother and a sister who were left at home while their mother went to work. Their mother wanted them to lock the door and not to let anyone in. The brother and sister did as they were told, but one day a tiger snuck its paw in through a window and said in a high-pitched voice: 'Open up. This is your mother. Unlock the door.'

"'I do not believe you are my mother,' said the little girl.

"'Feel my hands,' said the tiger, who was wearing soft white gloves. Its hands indeed felt like their mother's. The brother and sister ran to the window. The tiger was wearing a cotton dress similar to their mother's, but its tail was sticking out the back.

"'What do we do?' asked the little boy.

"'Run,' said the little girl."

My mother held me closer, changing her voice whenever she changed characters.

"The brother and sister ran outside and climbed a tall oak tree, all the way to the top, where they sat and watched the tiger. The tiger chased them but found it difficult to climb the tree.

"'Put sesame oil on your hands. It will help you grip the bark better,' the little girl called down to the tiger. But of course, the tiger could not grip the tree with oil on its paws.

"The little boy, who was not as clever as his sister, called down to the whimpering tiger, 'Use an axe.' The tiger ran to the children's home and grabbed their father's axe. When it returned, it started carving out footholds in the tree and began climbing. As the tiger neared the children, the little girl called out to the sky. As she did, she spied a magpie, a lucky bird.

"'Dear sky, if you want us to live,' she called, 'send down a brand-new rope. If you want us to die, send down a rotten rope that makes us fall.'

"A brand-new rope slipped down from a cloud, and the little boy and girl climbed all the way up to the sky and became the sun and the moon."

"What happened to the tiger?" I asked, hugging my knees in suspense.

"The tiger, who had heard the little girl's plea, also called out to the sky. It wanted to become the stars in between the sun and the moon. The sky dropped down a rotten rope. The tiger, which was even less clever than the little boy, had got the girl's words mixed up, and it thought that it could climb the old rope. It gripped the rope tightly and heaved its body around the rope with all its might, only to fall into the middle of a field of millet stalk."

"Oh," I sighed. "Poor tiger!"

"That is why," my mother continued, "in some parts of Chosun, whenever someone cuts into millet, the inside of the millet stalk is red, representing the tiger's blood."

I settled my chin on my knees and thought about the story. "If you are good and have a kind heart," I said slowly, "all your struggles and pain will be rewarded with what you want most. But if you are mean-hearted, you will fall to earth. I think that is what the story means."

"Do you?" asked my mother, her eyes flooded with tears. She wiped her damp cheeks, got up to make some rice and did not say another word to me.

Chapter Three

ON A DREARY afternoon in the sixth month of our second year in the mountains, as spring rain pounded like cows' hooves on our wooden plank roof, my father announced he was taking me somewhere.

It was a Wednesday, the one day he didn't go to the factory. Usually even when he was home, it was as if he wasn't there. He stayed in his room doing engineering sketches, wearing a face like stone whenever he emerged. What was conveyed through his silence was that my sister and I were our mother's responsibility, not his.

But this Sunday was different.

"Where are we going, Abuji?" I asked eagerly. Once I'd put on my navy-blue wool coat and red boots, my father slipped a plastic bag over my head. He'd cut holes in it for my nose and mouth, so I could breathe, and for my eyes, so I could see.

"Somewhere special," he said, his tone serious.

Water from the puddles in the road seeped through the holes in my plastic boots, soaking my feet. My toes were numb by the time we reached our destination.

Taking my hand, which he had never done before, my father pulled me around the corner and we emerged in front of a store.

We stepped inside and took off our rain gear. When I looked up, a woman, older than my mother and wearing a floral shirt and pants, gestured for us to enter.

My eyes moved to clotheslines stretching from one beam to another. T-shirts, slacks and wool sweaters hung from wooden clothes pegs. I noticed a pretty blue dress with a white lace collar that looked as if it would fit me. My heart beat faster. Was this why we had come? But the woman was unpacking things from some boxes in the corner and setting them on the floor.

My father picked up a box of red pencils. "Abuji, do you need these for sketching?" I whispered, as the woman put the other items away.

"No," my father said, handing the box to me. "I thought you might want to draw pictures when you listen to Chunbok and Manghil." He smiled. I smiled too. I had listened to the popular talk show at my grandparents' house since no one there ever paid me any attention.

"First thing though, as soon as I get home, I need to replace the speaker for the PA system so we don't miss a government broadcast," he explained. "Then, we can listen to Chunbok and Manghil."

My father pulled a small wad of won from his pants pocket and handed it to the old woman.

She wrapped the box of pencils in some paper.

"Where did you get the money in your pocket?" I asked my father as we put on our boots.

He winked. "You are a smart little girl. How do you know about money?"

"Well, I sometimes see Umma putting coins into a wooden box underneath the stove. She also showed me some won."

"I get some money from my job," my father explained. "I can use it to have your mother buy extra clothes or food items at government-approved stores like this one. The profits made at the store are given to the government. If anyone sells things privately, then they would be a capitalist."

BACK AT HOME, after my father and I had changed into dry clothes, he motioned for us all to gather around. He had re-placed the old speaker with the new one. At first, all we heard was static. But soon there were sounds: a car horn, a train whis-tle, a man talking in a gruff voice about the Japanese. Finally, a lone, deep male voice came through as clear as day. I mouthed the word to Umma: "Manghil!"

Manghil: We are on the farm. The time is monaegi, rice plant-ing, season. Ladies and gentlemen, hello. You're all really hard at work.

Chunbok: Can we finish all the work today?

Manghil: Of course, we can finish the whole plot in just half a day.

THE CONVERSATION BETWEEN Chosun's top personalities unfolded, with Chunbok and Manghil performing a little skit about how wonderful it was to feed the people of Chosun. I sat completely still, my heart full. They ended with a song. *"May is upon us, it is a beautiful season, let's go and plant rice, let's go and plant some rice."*

"When will I be old enough to plant rice, chili peppers and sweet potatoes?" I asked Umma as my father had turned the radio off. Scattered on the floor in front of me were my new pencils. On a piece of my father's white sketching paper, I had drawn pictures of vegetables.

"When you are at school," she replied.

"But when will that be?" I had been pestering my mother with this question since we arrived in the mountains but she had always changed the subject. Now she moved to sit beside me.

"I was a kindergarten teacher before you came into this world," she said quietly. "I will go back to being a schoolteacher when we return to Yuseon. But not until after..." My mother stroked her stomach. "After I have another baby."

"But we no longer have a home in Yuseon," I exclaimed, jumping up. "The government gave it to that other family when we moved here. Where will we live?" I didn't want to leave. I wanted to go to school in the building with the playground next door and ride on the *baeguneh* with my schoolmates. I had watched them with envy for so long.

"We'll live with grandma," my mother said.

I gasped. "Do you want that?" I asked, leaning in so my father wouldn't hear.

My mother blanched at my directness. "Whatever you feel about your grandparents," she answered after a long pause, "they are good, good people. Your grandfather is a leader, carrying out his revolutionary responsibilities. You must never say anything bad about them, ever."

MY BROTHER HYUNGCHUL was born in the late fall, just before Chunbok and Manghil announced on the radio that the harvest season had finished. Not long afterwards, my sister and I started packing up our pots, pans, bedding and pillows. On a chilly day in the twelfth month, when I could see my breath in the crisp air and my fingertips tingled in my thin woollen mittens, the gasoline car and the frog man returned to take us to the train station.

The journey went quickly. When we arrived at Yuseon, my father instructed my sister and me to stay where we were, nestled beside each other on the vinyl seats in the compartments.

Out the window, I could see people in dark factory clothes, their pace stiff and quick. Their drawn faces and heavy eyes revealed their exhaustion. In the mountains, everything had seemed to sparkle, even when charcoal clouds filled the sky. But everything in Yuseon was grey.

My eyes filled with tears. I didn't want to live with my grandmother. I didn't want to see my cousin Heeok. My sister, sensing my distress, touched my hand with her own sticky palm. "Big sister," she said. "You sad?"

I squeezed her hand and nodded. "Don't tell Abuji," I said softly, my spirits lifting.

My sister finally was growing up.

MY GRANDMOTHER'S HOUSE was one of the eight houses built together, with a front door painted the pale blue of a planting-season sky and sliding doors dividing the long and narrow house into three sections. While my mother unpacked our things in the room where we would sleep, I washed my grandmother's dishes, scrubbed the floors underneath the yellow paper and then swept the rooms reserved for her other sons and daughters when they came to visit. There were so many rooms, and my job, my grandmother told me, would be to clean them once a week. I wouldn't have time to play with my sister, I soon discovered. All I did was work.

When I was in the rooms farthest away from the main room, where my grandmother read the serials in the newspaper, I felt as if I was lost in a forest before dawn, with the mist drifting off the river. Every small noise on the streets outside made me jump. I swept slowly, alert to anything alive, including in the cobwebs I had to remove.

Although my mother and I did most of the cooking, my grandmother was clearly in charge. My halmuni had only to rub her stomach and my mother would put the new baby down and start boiling some rice with cabbage underneath. I dropped what I was doing to slice the cucumber while the white rice cooked. When she finally ate, she did it slowly, taking breaks to savour every bite. I watched with wide hungry eyes. My portions were smaller than they had ever been, and I could barely finish a few spoonfuls before my grandmother would order me to do another chore.

At night, my insides growled, keeping me awake. Pain ricocheted through my body. My stomach swelled from starvation. During the day, my head felt fuzzy, and my movements slowed. But I wasn't allowed to lie down. My grandmother would spank my bottom with the broom handle if she saw me doing anything except completing her list of chores.

After some time had gone by, my mother went back to her job as a kindergarten teacher, taking Hyungchul with her. She left him in the daycare located down the hall from her classroom. "Your school is not built yet," she told me. "When it is, then you will go."

One day, I followed Umma to the corner of the street, not wanting her to leave me alone with my grandmother. Sunyoung trailed behind me. My mother saw us out of the corner of her eye, stopped and turned.

I could see, even at a distance, that her lips were quivering, as if she was about to cry. Sunyoung gripped my shirt. Our bodies shook in the cool air.

"Come back," I yelled, raising my right arm toward her. But she turned away and resumed her walk to school.

WHENEVER MY GRANDPARENTS headed out to visit my cousins during the day, they would lock Sunyoung and me inside the house. Halabuji always locked the pantry, too, leaving Sunyoung and me with no food. As I listened to them walk away, I would bang my head against the door. My sister tugged on my tights, asking me what was wrong.

On those days when my grandparents were gone, often from morning until early evening, I'd race through my chores, my sister helping as best she could. Then we would lie down together on the ground and I would re-tell stories Umma had told me while my sister picked lice from my hair.

"There once were seven brothers who were left alone, a lot like you and me," I told her one day, as we pressed our bodies together under the duvet to keep warm. "One brother could see for a thousand *li*," I said, stretching my arms as wide as they would go. "The second brother could hear a whisper from a thousand *li* away. The third brother could lift an entire train with one hand. The fourth brother could travel a thousand *li* in a few footsteps. The fifth brother could breathe fire, and the sixth brother could smell fire from a thousand *li* away. The seventh brother could make himself small like an ant or as large as the biggest giant.

"These brothers were locked in their home all alone while their Umma and their Abuji worked. They were lonely. They didn't know what to do, until one day the strong brother ripped the door from its frame, and the brothers went out into the world.

"From that day on," I told Sunyoung, as she hung on every word, "the brothers helped the other villagers. The brother who could see such a distance spied on the rich, to learn who was greedy and who was a capitalist. He reported to the fast brother, who would race over to get the rich, greedy people's rice or cabbage and give it to those working hard in the factories, who needed more food for energy to work even harder. The brother who could smell fire alerted the strong brother, who would then fetch water from the well to put the fire out. The brother who could breathe fire made fires in the middle of the village to keep everyone warm in winter. The brothers worked together to help others."

"I like that story, big sister," Sunyoung said when I was done.

"We're like those brothers," I whispered, snuggling into her warm neck. "We just don't know yet how to get outside."

"I fly," Sunyoung said, flapping her arms. "Like sparrow."

MY COUSIN HEEOK had contracted rickets due to a vitamin D deficiency, my mother told me one evening. I was glad, though I concealed it. I hated Heeok so much for the candy and gifts she got from my grandmother that I no longer played with her. But I had noticed how she limped when she visited my grand-mother's house. Her legs were starting to resemble those of the frog man who drove the gasoline car. "Heeok is an *angibal*," I heard Halmuni say to Halabuji one night. "We need to help her, so she does not bring us shame."

"*Angibal* means a person with crooked feet," my mother ex-plained when we were alone. "If Heeok doesn't get better, she won't be able to work when she is older. The Party won't hire her. She'll be too slow, too weak, too broken. No one will want to marry her, either. Her rations will never grow because she will never get to work."

For the next few months, my grandmother paid a young man in the neighbourhood to go to a nearby city to buy wall-eye pollock. My mother would boil the fish, and at least three times a week my grandparents would spend the afternoon at my cousin's house, making sure she ate it. Their hope was that the oil in the fish would contain enough vitamin D to straighten out Heeok's legs.

One afternoon in the middle of the fifth month, just before

my seventh birthday and just after the birthday of our great father and eternal president, Kim Il-sung, my grandmother forgot to turn the key in the metal latch. I scurried over to the window and watched as my grandparents waddled down the street like the geese I'd see in the summer by the river. When they turned the corner, I grabbed my sister's arm and told her to put on her pants, and a jacket. Once we were dressed, we headed outside.

The ground was wet from planting-season rains. As my sister drew lines in the mud, I ran to the storage shed beside the house. My grandmother had left some of last season's cucumbers in a bucket of water. They had been frozen for the winter and the water was still icy cold, despite the warmer temperatures outside. I reached my bare hand in and pulled one out, yelling with pain as I bit into the skin. The cucumber was ice cold. But the shooting pain in my teeth and gums was not enough to stop me from eating it. I gave my sister one, too. After the cucumbers were gone, I lifted the plank of wood that covered the hole in the ground where my grandmother kept vegetables in summer and milk in winter. With my teeth, I pried open the cap on a bottle of goat's milk. I gulped down three quarters of it before handing the rest to my sister to finish. Just as I did so, a woman called out from the house next door, asking what I was doing. My body began to shake. The muscles in my legs and arms pulsed, as if my body wanted me to flee.

"Come here, child," she called out. "And bring your sister too."

I had never been inside anyone else's home, except that of a relative.

"Come with me," the woman repeated. But this time her tone was kind, and her two children had appeared and they were smiling. Sunyoung ran to them and was inside the house before I could decide what to do. I had to follow. I couldn't leave my little sister alone.

After the woman had taken off her jacket and helped her children out of their shoes, which I noticed were shiny and new, with not a single hole in the soles, she invited Sunyoung and me to sit. We crossed our legs and huddled together, enjoying the warmth from the *ondol* floor, the traditional heated floor with slabs of stone underneath warmed with hot air from the kitchen fireplace. As one of the boys unfolded the legs of a small wooden table, the other brought us steaming bowls of corn rice, followed by some noodles.

The two boys made shadow puppets with their hands on the wall. When she was done eating, Sunyoung joined them.

"Why are you not in school?" the woman asked me, sitting down and slipping on a pair of round spectacles.

"My umma said I was to start in the ninth month," I replied timidly.

She opened the large, red, leather-bound book she was holding. "It's by our eternal leader," she said, catching me looking at the cover. "It's about his life as a child. You must have a copy at your house," she continued as I nodded. "Would you like me to read you a story?"

I shook my head. I'd never had a conversation with anyone other than family members. I didn't know what to say or do.

When the light inside grew dim, and our neighbour's overhead light came on, I knew Sunyoung and I needed to head home. As soon as we were back in our yard, we each felt a hand swoop down and grab our coats. My grandmother hauled us inside the house.

"Where have you been?" she shouted. She didn't wait for a response. Instead, she grabbed me by the ear and dragged me into the second room, where she snatched a ruler. She hit me across the back of the legs so hard and so many times that I screamed out in terror.

I begged her to stop, but she aimed the ruler at my hands next. Soon my palms were covered in bloody scratches. Sun-young sat in the corner of the room, her eyes tightly closed, rocking her body back and forth. She had covered her ears to block out the sound of my cries.

"I never wanted you here," my grandmother yelled, her spittle landing in my hair. "You bring me shame by stealing my food. You and that mother of yours, your sister and you, you all bring me shame."

My halmuni stopped suddenly. I turned my head to see what she was staring at. My mother stood in the doorway, her face white, her body shaking like the ruler my halmuni held in the air.

Chapter Four

THINGS CHANGED AFTER that incident. One cloudy after-noon, my grandmother told my sister and me to put on our sweaters. Heook's energy was slowly improving, and apparently she had asked grandmother if I could come and play tag with her in the backyard. The air was crisp, filled with the scent of fresh rain and damp leaves unearthed by the melting snow.

My grandmother still ordered me to do chores. But she didn't leave us alone or lock us up anymore. She gave my sister and me a little extra corn rice or kimchi during mealtimes. In the afternoons, while she read, we were allowed to lie on our duvets and play hand-shadow puppet games. When spring fully emerged, we even went outside and made mud pies.

After work one night, my father announced that he had requested a new house, a home just for us. My grandparents, sitting off to the side, lowered their heads as we packed up our duvets and pots and pans and moved yet again.

Our new house was not far from my grandmother's place. Sunyoung and I would still spend our days alone, my mother informed us. I would be in charge of looking after my sister and making our meals. In the mornings, before she set off with Hyungchul, Umma would put the rice and some water on the stove for me to cook. She then locked us inside when she left.

Sunyoung and I spent our days making music with the pots and pans, dancing and singing at the top of our lungs. One afternoon, I dug a long piece of cloth from my mother's chest. I tied one end to the door handle of my father's drawing room and the other end to the pantry door. When we shut one door, the other would pop open. *Open, close, open, close . . .* we did this for hours.

By the end of the third week, though, these activities had lost their initial attraction. My sister would lie on a cotton mat and stare at the ceiling, while I looked out the window at the shed where my father kept our wood.

When my parents were at home, I was allowed to play in the shed. Through the holes in the wall, I would spy on the other neighbourhood children running around in their yards. I learned their games, including one where they tried to outsmart each other by shaping their hands like rocks, paper or scissors. I taught these games to Sunyoung, and we sometimes played them during our days locked indoors. But the fun lasted only a little while, and then we would fall idle again.

Sometimes my sister and I would amuse ourselves by playing ration shop. Sunyoung play-acted a mother, holding a blanket in her arms as if it were a real baby. I played the ration officer who checked the ration card and made sure that the correct amounts of food were handed out.

"I came to get the rations," Sunyoung would say.

"Here comes the rice—also pick up the potatoes," I said.

"Your family of five gets four kilograms of rice for a fortnight," I replied stiffly, just like I imagined the real ration officer would do. "But because you are a new mother and are breast-feeding, you can also get two kilograms of grain powder as well."

I also liked to look through my father's drawings, which were strewn across his desk or rolled into cylinders that stood upright in the corner of the room. In the shed were also various machine parts. I asked my mother what they were. She said Abuji was good at building machines. Indeed, in the evenings and on the holidays he would spend hours in the shed making things like a rice harvesting machine and a corn popper. Ships were his favourite subject to draw. I had never seen a ship in real life. My mother had explained that to the east was an ocean with water so deep that if I fell into it, I would never be seen again.

"HOW DID YOU and Abuji meet?" I asked Umma on one of her days off from teaching.

"A friend of mine had a husband who was a cousin of your father's. I was teaching school by then. Our friends introduced us."

ONE AFTERNOON IN my father's room, I picked up his fountain pen, grabbed a piece of scrap paper from the garbage and began drawing. The ink flowed from the pen tip onto the paper, reminding me of swallows' wings touching the sky. I drew a picture of my little sister, then did some of the alphabet letters my mother said I would be learning in school. Soon after, though, the pen broke.

I was so engrossed in what I was doing that I did not hear my father's footsteps as he came home from work early, suffering from a flu that made him feverish. I was trying to fix the pen but it was no use. I stopped only when I felt a tap on my shoulder.

My father stood, red-faced and still in the grey uniform he'd worn ever since I could remember. I didn't even wait for his words. I stood up on wobbly legs and turned around.

"Roll up your pants," he ordered.

With trembling hands, I rolled them up.

My father took the broomstick handle and smacked the backs of my legs three times hard.

A few days later, my mother announced that she'd now be taking Sunyoung to the daycare at her school. I was to spend my days now with my father, at his work. I'd be there until I started school in the ninth month.

AND SO I adopted a new daily routine. I would wake and dress immediately, eat a bowl of corn rice, and then hurry with my father to the train station. We travelled three stops to get to his factory, which was located on the outskirts of the city. The factory building was a simple white building with a dark metal roof. The workers were stiff looking, their eyes piercing forward, their shoulders proud, all wearing the same uniform as my father.

Abuji led me inside the building and through to the main area. He pointed at the high voltage warning signs next to the electric wires inside. A person who worked at the factory had gotten too close to those wires and been injured here, he warned me. "You need to listen, Sunhwa. You must never come into the factory floor on your own."

My father left me sitting in his supervisor's office. I had to wait there until break-time, he said, when he could join me. I sat down on the floor in the corner, pulled my legs tight against my chest and slowly scanned the barren room. It was large, with a furnace in the middle and a photo on the wall of our great father and eternal president, Kim Il-sung, wearing a black suit. We had the same photograph at home.

In my head, I told myself stories. After what seemed like a whole day, but was really just a few hours, my father returned.

"Come sit beside me," he said, patting a chipped wooden bench that at one point had been painted the Party's favourite colour, sky blue.

I crouched beside him as some Party members joined us. I felt shy. I had never been alone with a group of men.

My father, whom I had only seen smoking in our shed, took a package out of the breast pocket of his grey work shirt. I watched as he scraped pieces of tobacco into a piece of paper and then wrapped it into a small cylinder.

My father remained silent as the other men talked about the Party and the government. I chewed on some chives I had picked at a farm my father and I passed on the way to the train station. "Kim Il-sung is like the eternal flame of our stove fires," one man said. "A fire that never goes out and remains strong, despite the weather."

"Thank you, General," another man added, turning to the portrait of our leader on the wall. "Thanks to you we have such a good life."

I spent weekdays for the next few months in my father's supervisor's office, playing games in my mind. I often pretended to be the little girl in Umma's story, calling up to the sky for a rope so she could escape the tiger. "If I am meant to be anywhere but here," I chanted silently, "send me a good rope that I can climb."

I longed to be with the children I saw through the dusty window, chasing each other with their coats undone, their cheeks flushed, their faces bright with laughter. They attended the factory's kindergarten class. "Oh, sky," I thought to myself. "I won't ask so much as to become the sun or the moon, just one of the stars in between, if you send me a rope to help me escape this room."

Chapter Five

FOOD WAS SCARCER than ever for my family. My grandfather, my father told me, had retired from his position as a biology teacher, and my grandmother had stopped working as a music teacher when her own children were young. Their sons and sons-in-law supported them now.

One balmy summer day, my mother and I sat together on the ground while my father and sister tended the small patch of ground we had tilled, stretching from behind our house to a nearby river. My parents had planted potato and cabbage seeds soon after we moved in. That afternoon, Hyungchul toddled after the goat and the sheep my grandfather had lent us. My grandfather had raised the animals in his yard, but there was little grass left there for them to eat. They were both females and we would be allowed to keep their offspring.

"The Party gives extra rations to people like you and Abuji, who toil long and hard for our great father and eternal president," I said to my mother, who was picking burrs out of a sweater.

She nodded, not looking up from what she was doing.

"But Halabuji and Halmuni have so much more than we do because their sons also give them food."

"We share our food with them sometimes, but not always," my mother said matter-of-factly. "When your grandfather is in good health, he has work watching the melon fields. He gets extra food from the farms when he does this. It's our duty to help look after them when they are weak."

"But then we go hungry ourselves!" I blurted.

My mother spoke sharply. "Don't be disrespectful!" She stood up wiping earth from her navy-blue skirt.

"Wait," I said, tugging on the back of her tights. I was determined that day, whatever the cost, to get some answers. "Why is Halmuni so mean to us? Please tell me!"

My mother looked out over the field for a moment. I glanced at my shoes, covered in mud, and was ashamed of my boldness. But she surprised me by sitting back down.

"Your father has never told me much about his life," she began. "But he did confide that his umma was very spoiled. Your grandfather did everything for her, even sharpening her teaching pencils at night. Your grandfather did the housework, too, with the help of your father and his brothers and sisters. Your grandmother was the daughter of a corner-store owner. Your grandfather's father was a farmer, so when your grandparents wed, it was considered a good marriage for him. Back then, before our eternal father was in charge, farmers were not respected as they are today. Back then, capitalists were respected instead. Today, your grandmother's family would be seen as capitalists who take advantage of others. Your grandfather's family would be the virtuous ones for serving the Party."

I kept my head lowered as I pressed on. "But Halmuni is not mean to Heeok. She gives her candy and makes her fish oil. Why does she not like me?"

"Because you were my firstborn child and you weren't a son. Heeok has an older brother," my mother replied, after a long pause. "During Chosun's war with the puppet army of the Americans and their allies, your father's father was a member of the Labour Party, which later became the North Korean Workers Party. But there was a rumour on the street that members of the Party were going to be killed by security forces backed by the Americans. Your grandfather buried his membership card rather than wearing it around his neck. He didn't want to be identified. When the puppet army made it to Yuseon, where they lived, your grandmother fled with your father and his five siblings to another city, where they stayed in the home of a Party supporter. After the war ended, the family returned to Yuseon."

"I've seen the photos of Halabuji posing in his uniform," I said excitedly.

"Your grandfather went to find his card," my mother continued, "but he couldn't remember where he had buried it. Because of that, your father and your aunts and uncles all had trouble when they tried to register for membership in the Party. Your father received his Party membership card only when we moved to Suhdoosoo."

"Oh!" I exclaimed in shock. I had always assumed my father and his siblings were Party members.

"So that is why Abuji married me. Both our families had problems with the Party," she concluded. "Your father and I met only twice before we wed and your grandmother never liked me. She has always felt your father should have married better. Then, when you were born a girl, and not a treasured firstborn son, she cut off completely any feeling she might have had for you or me." My mother got to her feet, signalling the end of our conversation.

EVERY SATURDAY MORNING, my parents, like all workers, took part in *saenghwalchonghwa*, or total life retrospective. Each person present had to face their peers and document all the things they felt they had done wrong that week. My mother would confess that she had not pressed her skirts or shirts as well as she could have or shown enough respect to our great father and eternal leader. My father might admit to taking an extra-long cigarette break, as he sometimes liked to do. For their transgressions, my mother explained to me, people were forced to stand at the front of the main meeting room, head lowered, hands by their side, backs flush against the wall, while their colleagues stared at them.

My mother was always quiet and withdrawn when she returned. She would spend the rest of the afternoon by herself, reading one of the serials from the newspaper or mending the holes in our clothes.

Two Saturdays before school was due to start, however, my mother returned from saenghwalchonghwa in an upbeat mood. She got my brother ready and told Sunyoung and me that we were all going for a walk. She hummed a song as my sister and I skipped along beside her, something I had not heard her do since Sunyoung was a baby.

Our destination turned out to be someone's house. Inside, the walls of one room were lined with shelves piled with boxes of food, including biscuits and candies. Clotheslines dripped with shirts, dresses, pants and skirts. In another room, bookshelves and racks bulged with stationery items, cleaning supplies and make-up.

Umma asked the storekeeper, an older woman with a crooked smile, to bring out some skirts and tops she thought would fit me. My mother held them up to my body to gauge the size. She picked out a green plaid wool skirt, a white blouse, a solid green vest and a matching blazer. "For school," she said, as she handed the lady some won she had tucked in her pocket.

By the time we left the shop, I also had two new pairs of underwear, a pair of thick green socks, a handful of pencils and a red backpack, something my mother said all the children carried. I had never had so many things that were just mine before, and when we got home, I tore a piece of paper from the pad my mother had bought for herself and practiced my letters with one of my new pencils. That night, I slept holding the letters in my hand.

IN THE LAST few weeks before school started, the train to my father's factory seemed more crowded than ever. Every family, including ours, was receiving smaller food rations as we waited for the government to stock the shelves with vegetables from the autumn harvest. I didn't have to worry about teetering backwards and forwards with the motion of the locomotive since there were adults packed in all around me, holding me rigid like one bean sprout in the midst of many.

I was so hungry by the third day of accompanying my father to his work that my head felt light. The air was stuffy inside the train, and I had to lock my knees to stop myself from collapsing. If I fell, I knew I might be trampled. The next day, I picked two handfuls of chives at the farm we passed on our way to the train station, hoping the extra handful would give me extra energy.

But once I was on the train, the combined odours of perspiration, stale cigarette smoke and foul breath overcame me. I began to choke, gasping for fresh air. I put the chives to my nose, hoping the sweet smell would revive me, but my body began to shake. I sank to my knees, and everything around me started spinning. All I saw as I collapsed was the red lipstick a woman beside me was wearing. It was the same colour as Youngrahn's.

I WOKE AT home to the sounds of the well handle creaking up and down. I lifted my aching head to see Sunyoung lying near my feet, playing with a black sock she had placed on her hand like a puppet. She was talking softly, pretending to be a goat. "Bleet, bleet," she giggled. She took another sock, this one white, and slipped it over her other hand. "Baa, baaa," she said.

"You wake, big sister!" she squealed, when she saw my eyes were open. "Come play! Come play, big sister!"

"No," I said, shaking my head. My body was chilled, despite the warm day and the heavy duvet covering me.

My mother felt my forehead and then put another blanket over top of me. "You fainted," she explained. "I had to leave work. This is not good. You need to look after yourself better."

"Yes, Umma," I said, looking down at the duvet instead of into her eyes. "I promise."

"I'm going out," my mother said, tucking the duvet around my neck. "I'll get you some aspirin to help bring the fever down. Sunyoung will stay with you."

I awoke a few hours later, my head pounding, my legs and back aching. I was covered in sweat, and the inside of my mouth was pasty. I was so hungry that my stomach hurt. I ate the chives I still had in my pocket, but that made no difference.

I looked around the room. The walls of our home were off-white. There was a hole in the ceiling where the light fixture should have been. We were the first family to live in this house, and it had never been finished. We didn't even have a front door. My father had nailed a piece of canvas to the doorframe to keep the animals out. Abuji said the government would give us a real door before winter.

I closed my eyes and remembered a riddle my mother had once told me while we were planting.

"What stands in the middle of the farm with a baby on its back?" she had asked.

"The farmer's wife," I replied, thinking myself clever.

"No," she said mischievously.

"Maybe the farmer's mother?"

"No."

"I don't know," I finally shrugged.

"It's corn," she said, with one of her rare smiles. "Corn, standing tall in its tusk."

THE NEXT TIME I woke, I tried to pull myself up in bed, but I was too weak to do so. I rested my head back on the pillow. A shiver ran through me.

"Sunyoung," I called softly. "Sunyoung?"

A shadow crossed the window, making me jump. Then came the sounds of many footsteps. People were running into the backyard.

"Sunyoung," I heard someone else call.

More footsteps.

"Sunyoung, where are you?" I heard my mother call in a desperate voice that frightened me. "Sunyoung!"

I forced myself out of bed and ran outside in my bare feet. I was greeted by a parade of people, some heading into the forest as they called out Sunyoung's name, others running toward the river. Despite my fatigue, I found the strength to run with them.

In the stillness of the mornings in our house, when I woke before the others, I often heard the rapids of the river moving over the rocks. I would snuggle underneath the blankets, thinking of the fog that wrapped itself around the river's banks. I was glad to be at home and not near the water. Water scared me. I sometimes imagined myself sinking.

That day, as I hurried to the water with the others, I saw Sunyoung in my mind's eye, struggling against the force of the waves.

Just as I reached the riverbank, I tripped over a rock. As I stumbled forward, a strong arm swept me up.

"I don't want to lose two daughters in one day," Abuji scolded, setting my feet firmly on the ground. "Go back to the house. You're sick."

I looked around frantically. Men I recognized from the neighbourhood had climbed into the river and were plunging their arms beneath the surface. My heart beat so strongly in my chest that I thought I would faint again. I turned in one direction, then the other, not knowing what to do. All around me, people called out, "Sunyoung! Sunyoung!"

Suddenly my father was beside me once more. "Go back to the house," he ordered. "Go back to the house and let us look."

When I got back to our house, I sat down on a stone outside and cried, my head in my hands. I was supposed to watch Sunyoung. That was my job as a big sister. With my eyes still closed, I started punching myself in the head. "Bad, bad, bad! Bad big sister! Bad big sister!"

I felt a pat on my shoulder, but I could not pry my hands away from my eyes. I was too ashamed to face anyone.

"Big sister sleeping?" I heard a small voice ask.

I slowly opened my fingers and looked into Sunyoung's tear-stained face.

She was still wearing the sock puppets, and the white one was now muddy. "I wanted to play. You were sleeping, so I walked far, far, far looking for a friend," she explained, pointing to the mountains behind our house. "I got lost."

I screamed to let the searchers know that Sunyoung was home. When my mother neared, she started lecturing my sister for running away. "I told you to stay close to the house," she scolded. But she couldn't maintain her anger for long. She whisked my sister into her arms and began to cry with relief.

Even when my father said later that night that it was not my fault, I blamed myself for not watching Sunyoung. No matter what, I was her big sister. I was supposed to look out for her and protect her.

Chapter Six

THERE IS A tradition in Chosun in which families soak potatoes in pails of water from the time they are harvested until the
following summer. Just as the *deulgukhwa* were blooming, my
mother brought our pail in from the pit in the ground where
she had stored it and where the potatoes had remained frozen
for the winter. We spent an evening together peeling the potatoes, and the next morning, using a heavy stone grinder she had
borrowed from a neighbour, my mother ground the potatoes to
powder. On certain summer nights, we would meet at a neighbour's house with lots of other families. The neighbour would
take the powder everyone had brought and put it into a noodle
machine. Then my umma and the other mothers would cook
the noodles in big pots on open outdoor fires.

These were the only nights of the year when I knew for sure
that my belly would be full. We were supposed to feast on rice
cakes on Kim Il-sung's birthday, the fifteenth day of the fifth
month, but we rarely did because we couldn't afford to buy
them. Kim Il-sung's birthday was also an occasion on which we
were rationed pork. Even so, the meat we received was enough
to feed only one person, not all of us.

On potato noodle nights, I played hide and seek with the

other children on our street. At midnight, I would still be awake, lying on my mat, my stomach full, my legs tired from all the running, listening to the distant calls of wolves in the hills.

The weekend after Sunyoung's disappearance, someone called for a noodle night. On that night, however, I didn't play with the other children. Everyone stared at me as I walked beside my mother, Sunyoung on the other side. My mother gave our remaining powder to the older woman with the grinder. "*Jal mugssumnida*, I will eat this well," the woman said, as was customary.

I bowed politely, my face red with shame. I felt everyone knew I was a bad big sister. My mother had said it was not my fault that Sunyoung had run away. I was not responsible since I had been sick. But I felt I had let her and Sunyoung down nonetheless.

Sunyoung and Hyungchul, now a toddler, ran off to play with some of the other children. I sat on a stump and listened to the adults talk. Mostly the conversation revolved around our great father and eternal president. But then, as the crescent moon of August crept up from the horizon, and fireflies flickered their lights near the river, some of the men began to talk in whispers.

"The *Boweebu*—the security bureau—came and took her away," I heard one of them say. I inched my body closer, eager to hear more.

"She was going to the mountains and sending codes to the south," someone else said.

"She was a spy!" one man exclaimed, shaking his head.

"She was not loyal to our great father and eternal president," my father interjected, clicking his tongue.

Everyone nodded.

"She's in prison now," continued the man who had brought up the subject.

"What is her name?" I thought to myself, hugging my knees to stop myself from leaping up and yelling the question out loud. "Who are you talking about?"

"Her father was a capitalist. Her head was never right."

"She has a son," I heard my father say. "About Sunhwa's age."

"Who could it be?" I wondered, my mind going over all the children I saw at noodle night.

"I hope the son and his father have told the Boweebu that they do not support the woman," another man said.

Everyone nodded again.

That night, I could not sleep. I listened to the crickets rubbing their legs together, my eyes wide open as I stared into the dark. My head hurt from the way my mind kept churning over all my fears: fears that someone who lived close to us was a traitor.

THE NIGHT BEFORE I started school, my mother washed my hair and body with laundry soap. I cleaned the dirt from underneath my nails with the same wooden stick I used to pick lice.

The following morning, I woke before the others did and tiptoed over to the wall, where my father had nailed a peg for my clothes. I felt grown up. The top pegs held my mother and father's clothes, the bottom peg mine, including my school uniform. I ran to the outhouse and dressed after washing my hands. I couldn't eat my rice that morning, though, because my stomach was queasy from nerves. As I waited for my mother to finish eating, I squished my feet into my new black leather shoes, tossed my backpack over my shoulder and waited for her outside.

When my mother and I arrived at the school, we were instructed to stay in the yard with the other mothers and daughters. I gripped my mother's hand as we stood underneath a tree. There were four Grade 1 classes, two all-boys' classes and two all-girls' classes, my mother explained. As we waited for the school official to tell me where to go, I spied on the people around us. Some of the mothers wore navy skirts and high-heeled black shoes and had their hair in tidy buns. These women looked clean beside my mother. Their daughters, whom my mother said would also be in Grade 1, were twice as tall as I was. The fathers and mothers of those girls must hold important jobs in the Party, I thought, for some girls had bellies that looked like they might explode. I squeezed my mother's hand tighter and tried to duck in behind her. "If I get into a fight with one of these girls," I thought to myself, "I will surely lose."

I started to tremble as my mother released my hand. My name had been called, and a school official was escorting me to the line for my class. I closed my eyes tight and made a wish that I would end up with the girls who were my height and skinny. In the end, that was what happened. The larger girls were in the other class.

THE SCHOOL OFFICIAL had us walk single file to our new classroom, then sit on the floor cross-legged, facing the photograph of Kim Il-sung on the wall. After the bell rang three times, our teacher arrived. We called her *Sunsangim,* an honorific title indicating a person with great power. Once she had introduced herself, she proceeded to guide us in what would become a morning ritual: a dedication to our great father and eternal president.

"The beloved father is watching over you," Sunsangim told us. "So sit upright and behave properly."

She then recited a story from Kim Il-sung's childhood: "Once our great father and eternal president's straw shoes were falling apart, and his mother gave him money she had saved from sewing for new shoes. She told him to buy the best rubber shoes at the market. But instead, he bought new shoes for his mother."

"Ohhh," I hummed silently. "He is such a good man."

"We must try to be like him," Sunsangim concluded.

"Once our great father and eternal president's mother fell ill," Sunsangim told us another day. "She needed a special fruit from a distant mountain. Only that fruit, a prune, would cure her. Kim Il-sung, just a young boy at that time, went in search of the fruit. He walked for days with no water or food. On the brink of starvation, he found the fruit, and he saved his mother."

Now that I was in my first year of school, I vowed to dress nicely, to write neatly, to do well in my studies, to be thoughtful to others and, when someone was in trouble, to help them. I wanted to possess all of the virtues of Kim Il-sung. "I want to be like him," I told my umma that night.

"I want to be just like our great father," I told the stars as I stared out the window.

From my first school day on, I said, "Thank you, dear father," whenever I passed in front of the eternal president's portrait in our home. I said, "Thank you, dear father," before every meal. "Thank you, dear father," I recited after every good mark I received in math or Korean lessons. "Thank you, dear father," I muttered every night before hopping under the duvet and nestling my head next to Sunyoung's.

In the mornings, when our class leader went to the front to lead us in the oath of allegiance to our eternal president, I was determined to stand straighter than anyone. My voice, I vowed, would carry the most dedication. "I promise to study hard, to model harmonious group behaviour and to pay allegiance always to our beloved father. I swear I will," I recited.

In the song that followed, I opened my mouth wide, articulating everything with perfect pitch: "Our leader, standing atop Goonhaham Rock, takes out from his sheath a general's sword. We have victory over our enemies! He takes out the sword, and at the sound of the sword, unleashed from the sheath, the Japanese tremble."

The autumn days turned crisp, and the biting winds snapped at my cheeks. I read the textbooks on Kim Il-sung's childhood in the dim light of our house until my eyes closed and my head toppled forward onto the pages.

Every night before bed, I took a cloth and dusted the frame around the portrait of Kim Il-sung, as Sunyoung looked on. When I was done, we would both bow and say: "Thank you, father."

NEAR THE END of my first year, Sunsangim divided us into groups of four and had us line up shortest to tallest. I was a year older than the other students, because I had been started late, but I was still one of the tiniest, so I was very upset when the teacher placed me at the front of one of the lines. The child behind me, a short wide girl with a round face, stuck her tongue out at me when Sunsangim wasn't looking. "We're shorter than you," she whispered into my ear, pointing to herself and the two other girls. "But you have to go first."

The other girls pointed at me and stuck their tongues out, too. Anger bubbled up from deep inside me. I felt like hitting the girl behind me.

As Sunsangim explained the activity, my anger subsided. We were to run to the wall on the far side of the room and then back.

"*Yoy, ddang* —ready, go," the teacher said. I leapt forward, running with my head high, my arms pumping, my legs the longest gait I could stretch them into.

"I am going to come first and show those girls that being of service to our eternal president is the only way to live," I vowed, as I kept my eyes focused on the chalkboard on the other side of the room.

Suddenly, I crashed into a cement chair placed to divide the two sides of the room. The blow sent me backwards with such force the air was knocked out of me. I landed on my back with a thud and started choking.

A few of the girls stopped running, but the teacher waved for them to finish. Sunsangim came to my side and told the teaching assistant to fetch my mother, who was in the kindergarten a few classrooms over.

As my breathing returned to normal, the teacher lectured me. "You were not looking. You were too focused on the goal you would achieve. The chair was placed there to see who would falter."

I wanted to apologize, but all I could do was stutter.

"You were consumed with your anger, too," she continued. "You were not thinking clearly. You allowed your emotions to cloud the purpose of the work you needed to achieve."

I gasped at her words.

"I see much even when I am not looking," she said, answering my unspoken question. "You have failed our great father today."

I glanced at the girl with the round face, my face steaming again in anger. Her father, I had heard, was a factory supervisor, a loyal and devoted Party member. "I will always be an outsider," I thought to myself, my heart heavy. I wanted to cry beneath the classroom portrait of Kim Il-sung, begging him for his forgiveness.

Chapter Seven

DURING THE SUMMER holidays between my first and second year of school, which stretched across the eighth month, my mother decided to take my sister, my brother and me to her parents' house in Hoeryong. Umma was pregnant again, the baby set to come near the end of the twelfth month. Unlike in her other pregnancies, Umma was tired all the time and could keep little food down. She vomited after nearly every meal. The only thing that agreed with her was corn rice, and only if she ate it right before bed.

Whenever my siblings and I had a fever or a winter cough that stayed in our chests for weeks, my mother would worry that she had caused it. She had not been given the seaweed soup or white rice after our births that would make her breast milk full of nutrients and vitamins. "Your father and I couldn't afford these things from the black market," she told us. Because she believed her own milk was deficient, she had weaned us early, feeding us goat's milk instead. None of us were truly healthy, and my mother said we hadn't had the right start in life. Anything bad that befell us was because of her, she believed. She was not a good mother.

That summer, my mother was worried that the child inside

her would not live. That was the reason we were going to her umma and abuji's farm, she told us. They had so much food, and my mother would have help with us so that she could rest.

THE LAST TIME we had visited Hoeryong was in the first month of that year. My abuji had come too, for a few days' holiday. It had been very cold and we needed to bundle up. All that showed above my scarf were my tiny black eyes when my father, my sister and I tried tobogganing. We abandoned our outdoor fun to head inside, but it was not much warmer there, even by the stove. My grandfather pulled the squashes he had harvested in the fall out of storage. My sister and I cut them open and then into slices, which my halmuni baked. Once we had eaten the flesh of the squash and the seeds and had licked our fingers clean, we all felt warm inside. That night, the full moon had shone across the virgin snow, causing the shadows to dance.

From our earlier visits, I knew that in springtime Hoeryong was covered in white apricot blossoms. The air would be full with their powdery scent, and their fuzz floating in the air. To me, Hoeryong was a city of lights, with crimson-lipstick smiles on women with perfect teeth and men with rosy cheeks who bowed ever so slightly when they passed my parents on the street.

"This is the hometown of the tireless eternal fighter and revolutionary comrade, the wife of Kim Il-sung," a female voice announced as we disembarked at the main station. "Welcome to Hoeryong."

I was tired, since we had left home in the middle of the night. I could barely move my legs, let alone carry my bottari, which contained a few changes of underwear and some rice. We could not afford to hire a car, so we walked to my grandparents' farm. The cement houses in the main city and the sandy-dirt road were a blur. My legs dragged, my head slipping to one side as my eyes closed.

But as soon as the road widened and I saw the swallows dipping in and out under the apricot trees, I woke up. I knew we were close to our destination.

My maternal grandfather had retired from his job at a factory, where he had worked with amputees from the war. Now he was a watch guard for a farm run by many families, and he brought home lots of food. My grandmother also maintained a farm, on which she grew scallions, chili peppers for kimchi, eggplant and cucumber. As we walked past the apricot trees, planted so evenly they looked like schoolchildren lining up for an assembly, my mouth watered. We often starved at home, our rations failing to last. But not at my grandparents' house, whether in winter or summer. There we feasted.

I ALSO FELT wanted at my mother's parents' house. From the time I was a tiny child, just learning to walk, I would hide in one of the cupboards as soon as I arrived. Everyone, including my aunts and uncles, would drop what they were doing to look for me.

"Where am I?" I would call out to my halmuni when I spied her through the crack in the door.

Borimahnti means pig, or a gluttonous girl. "Where is that borimahnti?" my umma's sister Hyegyung would call, clapping her hands to her face and squealing as she opened the cupboard door and looked into my eyes. She would always pretend she had not seen me and shut the door.

"Oh, borimahnti," she would call out. "Oh, borimahnti, where are you?"

When I finally emerged on my own, my mother's family feigning that they had given up the search, my aunt would ruffle my hair and smile while my halmuni pretended to chide me. "You had us so scared, so very scared that we would never be able to find you," she would say.

That afternoon, my grandmother served a meal as soon as we reached the farm. I gobbled down my food so fast I had moved on to seconds while Halabuji and Halmuni were only halfway through eating.

After three bowls of rice, I ran outside to climb an apricot tree. When I had gone as high as I dared to go, I picked some fruit and sucked out the juice. Sunyoung moaned from below that she wanted to join me.

"Climb!" I called out. "Climb."

"But I don't know how," she cried. "Help me!"

"Put your feet in the ridges in the bark," I called, juices from the fruit dripping down my chin. "Remember the tiger story? Your courage is your rope. Just open your eyes and climb."

I continued eating as Sunyoung struggled up to join me. Every now and then she would cry out in terror or pant from her efforts. When she was nestled beside me, sucking on apricots, I softened. "I like it here best," I confided.

"Me too, big sister," she said.

"I wish we lived here."

When we returned to the house, my mother and my halmuni were seated cross-legged on the floor, reading books they had bound themselves with thick tape, using serial stories from the *Hahmbook Ilbo* newspaper of Kim Il-sung's life.

"What does it say?" I asked my grandmother, stretching out beside her on my stomach. I felt full for the first time in a long time.

"This one is called the *Outskirts of Baekdu Mountain*," my halmuni answered. "Our great father and eternal president Kim Il-sung is said to have been born there. The main characters are

Jang Chuljoo and Myung Hyuk, a man and his wife, and their small child."

My mother picked up the tale. "There are actually four people in the story, and they all make military uniforms," she continued. "Everyone is starving from the Japanese occupation, digging up whatever herbs and roots they can find to eat."

"The book is set in the 1930s, Sunhwa-ya," my halmuni said. "Very old. Very old. Long before you were born. Long before . . . " Her voice and her eyes drifted, and her hands started to tremble. My mother had told me after our last visit that my grandmother had the shaking disease that affected so many old people.

"But despite their hunger, the couple dedicate their lives to the dream of liberation from the Japanese," my mother concluded, taking over for her mother. "They are an example of how we are all supposed to live."

THE NEXT MORNING, after bowls of white rice, I felt so happy to be in the countryside, eating whatever I wanted, that I started to sing.

"In order for flower buds to blossom, he gives, he gives, he gives us this warm sunshine. Thank you, eternal father. Thank you."

"What song is that?" Sunyoung asked as we walked with our grandfather and Umma on the paths between the fields.

"It's the song from school," my mother hummed, her eyes shining. She began to sing along with me in her lovely strong voice.

"Maybe you're a singer, too!" my halabuji said to me when we were done.

"No," my mother said sharply, her smile gone.

"But Sunhwa-ya sings like you. Maybe you can tell her teacher, and she can be placed on the singing team."

"No," my mother said sternly. "She can never sing at home, never."

"I'll sing you a song, then." My grandfather leaned over and winked, distracting me from my mother's sudden change of mood. *"Gold child . . . once the gold child was riding a horse on the way to the market. He fell off and into a stream."* He repeated the same two lines over and over.

I giggled. "What a silly song. Where did you learn it?"

"Don't ask such things," my mother hissed.

"Ah, Sunhwa-ya," my grandfather whispered, "it's a song from before the revolution."

"Oh," I replied, eager to learn more.

He laughed, a deep guttural sound. "The first song I learned after liberation was about Kim Il-sung and the south mountain. It is more like a ballad. *"The green pine trees in the South Mountain are persecuted through the bitter winter; mired under the snow and frost. The balmy and warm spring will come back, and we'll come back to life. Do you know that it will come back to life when the warm spring comes back, do you know my people? Do you know my people? Even though we have been through so much, in springtime it will come back to life."*

While he sang, my grandfather's hands and arms swooped through the air. When he was through, he pointed at my mother but looked at me. "This song is better for you!"

"Yes," my mother agreed stiffly.

"It was a song composed by our great father and eternal president's father, Kim Hyong-jik," my grandfather said to me. "It means that the Korean people who were persecuted under the Japanese occupation are to have hope. They will have spring again."

CHAPTER SEVEN

ONE MORNING WHEN Sunyoung and Hyungchul were so lazy their eyelids dropped and thunder clapped outside, eventually sending down a rain so heavy it created deep ruts in the muddy earth, I decided to explore the many cupboards my grandfather had built into his home.

I opened one small closet, coughing on the particles of dust and rubbing my stinging eyes. When my eyes cleared again, I was looking at shelves piled high with cameras, lenses and containers with words on them I could not read.

"Ehem!" I jumped and turned quickly to face my grandfather, who was standing at the closet door.

"I'm so sorry," I said, bowing, then trying to skirt past him.

"Sunhwa-ya, it is fine. I am glad you discovered my little secret. Come, let me show you." He turned on an overhead light that shone red and then shut the door.

"I used to be a photographer. A war photographer," he said, picking up a camera and letting me look through a tiny hole. I could see my grandfather's nostrils at the other end.

"Once, when I was in the middle of a field with people dying around me, I couldn't take the suffering anymore. I walked to a river. There was an apple vendor—his body had been ripped to pieces by bullets," Halabuji continued. "I closed my eyes and aimed my camera, shooting, shooting, shooting. I turned my lens on the river. There were apples floating, bobbing in and out of the corpses. We were all so hungry," he said, wiping his eyes. "I started picking up the apples to take home to your halmuni and umma. I was wrong to do this. I lost my senses. I cared not for the dead but just for the living."

I didn't know what to say, so I looked down at my slippers.

"Hoeryong was bombed during the war. We endured endless air raids that shook the beams of our houses and left sick

69

and dying people littering the streets. Your grandmother, who loved to sing and dance, fell quiet. She would sit in the corner like a child, holding a pillow and rocking herself back and forth.

"One bomb landed right next door, destroying our neighbour's house. We ran in every direction. Your grandmother had gone to grab her youngest child, who was just a baby. But once we had made it to the hills and were reunited, your halmuni opened her arms, and in them, she was carrying only a pillow."

I gasped. "What happened, Halabuji?"

"She had left the baby in the house, and we couldn't return for a full day due to the fighting. The South Koreans and the Americans were everywhere, dropping bombs and killing people."

"What happened?" I whispered, grabbing my grandfather's pant leg and tugging on it.

"When we returned, the city was black from the smoke of the fires, even though it was mid-morning. The house beside our own was nothing more than ash."

"No," I gasped, pinching my eyes shut. "The baby was killed!"

"Halmuni has never been normal since," my grandfather said, his own face wet with tears. "That look she gets in her eyes, you know, where she drifts off and her body begins to shake, and then her eyes become frantic."

I nodded.

"Well, that look and the pacing she does, that is what she did when she saw the burned house. But Sunhwa-ya, the baby didn't die."

"How?" I exclaimed.

"I don't know. I saw a tiny sparrow land on the roof of our house just as I pushed open the door, which had been blown off its hinges. And inside was your aunt Hyegyung, sucking her knuckle, lying in her own filthy diaper. But she lived." My grandfather wiped his face with his hands. "You can look in this room whenever you like, but never touch the chemicals up there," he said, pointing to the containers on the shelves. "Those are for developing photos, and they are poison."

ON ONE OF the last days of our holiday that summer, I decided to trick my halmuni. She was in a particularly good mood, humming the revolutionary songs I had been teaching Sunyoung while she made us porridge, then hanging the duvets over the clothesline to air.

I snuck into my grandfather's special closet as I saw Halmuni about to sit down and read one of her serial books. I grabbed one of the containers I was forbidden to touch and walked towards my grandmother.

"I'm going to eat this for lunch!" I said to her.

My grandmother leapt up, dropping her book on the floor. She stepped on it, crumpling a few pages as she rushed toward me. She pointed a shaking arm. "Sunhwa-ya, give me that."

"No," I replied, taking a few steps backwards. A grin slid across my face as I pretended to open the lid. "I'm going to eat this," I taunted.

"Sunhwa-ya," my grandmother pleaded, her eyes now teary. "Please stop." Her legs collapsed, and she fell to the floor.

I was contrite. "It's a trick," I said, putting the container down and running to her side. "I would never hurt myself. I'm sorry I scared you."

"I don't want to lose another child," she said softly, her eyes darting back and forth, her body trembling.

"But you never lost a child," I stammered.

"Yes," she said, her eyes staring out at nothing. "The house burned. The baby died. I am a bad mother."

It was hard to leave Hoeryong and my grandparents after that golden summer. As we drew close to Yuseon on our train ride home—the cement houses, the streets upon streets of apartment buildings in which Party officials lived, the rows of factories with their black metal gates, the endless low-rise homes in the suburbs—my world turned grey, even though the sun shone.

Chapter Eight

"DAECHUL AND HIS father have been taken away by the Boweebu," my friend Sumi told me, pulling me aside in the schoolyard as I arrived for the first day of classes.

"No," I exclaimed, placing my hand on my chest. I wondered what the Boweebu, the state secret department, would do to a child not much bigger than me. "What for?"

"Daechul's mother was a spy. She was put in prison last summer. Didn't you know?"

I sighed with relief. "I heard some men talking, but I didn't know who they meant. I feel better now. We're safe."

By now another friend, Mihwa, had joined us. "She betrayed the revolution and our great father, Kim Il-sung. She got what was coming to her."

"What do you think the Boweebu will do to them?" I asked.

"I don't know," Sumi said. "It's a bad family."

"I saw a movie once about prison," Mihwa said. "The cells were dark, and the people were hung upside down by their feet and tortured."

"How were they tortured?" Sumi asked, her eyes wide, eager to learn the details.

"The guards used whips and chains to beat them on their backs and their legs."

I shook my head to drive away the image. On noodle nights, Daechul would smile and run faster on his stocky muscled legs than children twice his size. Earlier that summer, though, his face had become sullen, his eyes surrounded by dark circles. His movements had slowed. He had lost so much weight that his ribs poked out underneath his sweaters. I should have realized, I chastised myself, that Daechul was the boy about whom the men had been speaking.

I had felt safe earlier, but my relief was short-lived. "Anyone could be a spy," I thought, looking around the playground.

My anxieties grew as the days went by, and I started to get headaches from worrying so much. I was constantly tired, and I became slower at everything I did, including my homework and my chores. A few times the goat kicked me for falling into her or nicking her skin with the edge of the can as I was milking her. Once, I stood up and kicked her back, spilling the milk I had collected. I fell behind in completing my math exercises and copying out phrases in Korean to help me with my penmanship. As I struggled to finish my homework in the mornings, my mother would leave for work, not wanting to be late herself. I was left alone, often arriving at school after lessons had already begun.

I tried to listen to the teacher once I got there, but her words all ran together. All I could think about was sleep, spies and prison.

"I HOPE THIS cheers you up," Umma said as we settled onto hard metal chairs about halfway down the aisle of the movie theatre. It was the first time I had ever been to the cinema. It was an overcast late afternoon, and my mother had said she could not take any more of me walking around the house under a dark cloud.

The film was *The Flower Girl*, written, my mother whispered as the lights dimmed and a beam of light hit the wall in front of me, by our eternal father Kim Il-sung.

The screen came alive with moving pictures of a young woman, wearing a traditional *chima* and *jeogori* with a bow, walking through the mountains and picking purple and pink azaleas. All of a sudden, she was in a city, selling the flowers. I slid forward in my chair.

"You," said an old man with a long white beard to the flower girl, "will meet a nobleman."

But the film was not so happy. The flower girl's little sister, no older than Sunyoung, wanted to look at something that was burning in a long rectangular box. The landlady slapped the tiny girl so hard she fell backwards, hitting a boiling pot of water. The water splattered into her eyes, blinding her.

I jumped up and screamed. My mother told me to shush and urged me back into my seat. But I continued to sob.

The film was set just before the revolution. The flower girl's family was very poor, and they lived in a shed that belonged to their landlord.

"What is a nobleman?" the flower girl eventually asked her mother.

"They say a nobleman helps the poor like us, to make us rich," her mother replied. "If only such a man were to appear to you, as if in a fairy tale."

At one point in the film, the flower girl sang:

"*Every spring the hills and fields bloom with beautiful flowers, but we have no country, no spring. When will flowers bloom in our hearts, on the hill path Brother was dragged along? Spring comes and flowers bloom every year.*"

The flower girl's mother died following that, and her blind sister nearly did, too. But her brother, who had been imprisoned seeking revenge against the landlord and his family for blinding their sister, escaped and became part of the revolution. In the end, the flower girl's nobleman is her brother, who helps to liberate Chosun from the Japanese.

I cheered and cheered, my joy filling the theatre, when the peasants overtook the landlords.

ON SATURDAY MORNINGS, just as my parents did at their work places, I went to school to take part in saenghwalchonghwa. I had a Life Reflection Journal, and, in it I had to record all of my transgressions for the week. I would flip through my book of Kim Il-sung's quotes, choose one to copy out and then write my life for that week in review like this:

> Great Leader Kim Il-sung said as follows: Study is a battle. To a student, studying is the foremost duty and is a matter of life and death.
>
> This week, my uniform was wrinkled. I didn't have time in the morning to use the big iron to smooth down my pleats. I was late for school twice. I kicked the goat when she kicked me. I didn't play with Sun-young or tell her a story. I must try harder to be a better person.
>
> Great Leader Kim Il-sung said as follows: The oppressed people can only liberate themselves through struggle. This is a simple and clear truth, as confirmed by history.

My little baby brother, Hyungwoo, who was born in

the first month instead of the twelfth when he was scheduled to come, was crying. But instead of rocking him, or trying to get him to stop, I put my hands over my ears and continued what I was doing, rewriting a poem. I was not a good daughter. I did not help my mother.

I faithfully recorded all my transgressions each week for the saenghwalchonghwa with one exception. My greatest travesty was never divulged, not even by classmates who knew of my secret. Since watching my first movie, *The Flower Girl*, I had been consumed by the images I saw on the screen. At first, in my dreams, I saw the flower girl as she walked in the snow in her shoes made of straw. Even at school, when I should have been focusing on my studies, I imagined the work camps where prisoners were forced to carry big blocks of wood on their backs, blocks so heavy that blood flowed down their faces.

Children were not allowed to go to the cinema without an adult. But I soon learned to sneak in through the back, when the theatre was dark and the guards were not looking. The first movie I saw on my own was the love story *Chunhyangjeon*. I sat in the second row, my body hunched down in my seat, glancing around the theatre after every scene to make sure the guards hadn't seen me. As the movie ended, with the lights still low, I snuck back outside.

A week later, I took Sumi and Mihwa with me to see *Chunhyangjeon*. We snuck in the same way, huddling together in our seats and looking around every so often to avoid capture. No guards came.

Once I was confident I would not be caught, I allowed myself to attend the movies often and to fall in love with the stories. And once film had entered my life, I became inspired again.

My fuel was the dream that one day I would tell stories myself. For a while, I returned to doing my assignments promptly at school. I penned poetry and wrote short stories. I imagined my characters and storylines coming alive on film.

At first, all of my poems and prose were about devotion to Kim Il-sung. But then, when I was fourteen, I discovered my father's romance novels, tucked away in the bottom of one of his chests. I dove into them immediately, reading avidly.

"The couple's eyes met across the crowded room at a concert. The man, a loyal soldier in the military, gave his closest friend a message, written on paper, to give to the woman. The friend gave it to the woman's sister."

In one of the books, the two messengers also fell in love.

I would read these books secretly until I heard the door creak open to signal my father's return from work. Then I would quickly slip them back, imagining as I drifted off to sleep at night what it would be like to be kissed.

My years at school passed in these ways. Ever since Grade 6, I had been one of four girls regularly singled out for mutual critique, another part of saenghwalchonghwa.

In the mutual critique, a girl in the class chose another girl as the one who had committed the most wrongs that week. Both girls stood, and then the accuser outlined for the accused everything bad that she had done. Almost always, I was criticized for doing exactly what I had written in my Life Reflection Journal.

"Comrade, you are late for school and disrupt the class," one of the taller girls, with whom I barely spoke, said to me as I hung my head in shame. "And your uniform is wrinkled."

I looked down at my pleats. Even though we had been given new uniforms the year before to celebrate Kim Il-sung's birthday, I could never get my green pleated skirt to look like it had when I first received it.

"And your socks are dirty," my classmate scolded, pointing at my legs.

It was true. I only had two pairs of socks, and I often ended up wearing the same pair for weeks at a time. In spring my socks had mud on them from my walks home, and in autumn pieces of leaves stuck in them, from when I rolled down the hills.

"Comrade, you fall asleep in class," a large student told me at the end of one week. "And you didn't sweep the classroom when you were supposed to. You had your comrade do it."

All of it was true. I had started off my school years wanting to be an example for my great father Kim Il-sung but I had turned into a lazy adolescent. As I once wrote in my Life Reflection Journal:

> Communal living is like a firepot for refining your ideology . . . it is also the school for revolutionary thoughts— Kim Il-sung.
>
> My mother has four children. She can't look after everyone every single minute of the day. But I am not a good daughter. When my mother wants me to go to school, my bones and muscles are slow moving, I can barely tug my socks over my feet. I am always late for school, because I am slow at everything I do.

One movie that made a deep impression on me was *The Fire Spreading Around the World*. It was about Kim Il-sung's uncle, who was tortured by the Japanese during their occupation of Korea. I thought about Daechul, the neighbourhood boy, throughout the film. We had never seen him again, and we heard his entire family had been sent to a concentration camp.

In the film, the Japanese tortured our great leader's uncle by forcing him to stand outside on cold winter days. Water was thrown on him, and icicles formed on his face. He was also forced to walk over a burning hot iron plank and a bed made of sharp nails. Tears dripped down my cheeks as I watched the images on the screen. Anger grew inside me as it had when the flower girl's sister was blinded by their landlord. But when I imagined the Boweebu doing similar things to Daechul and his mother and father, I didn't feel the same rage. They deserved their torture, I believed. They were not loyal.

In my revolutionary history classes at school, I was learning about the brutal thirty-six years of Japanese occupation, during which Korean capitalists enslaved workers and Korean landlords profited from the blood and sweat of farmers. Landlords and capitalists were the most evil people in the world, we heard. Landlords beat their tenants, deprived them of food and then sold the girls to horrible men in the pubs. Capitalists, who ran the industrial plants, treated workers badly and stole our country's natural resources, including iron and magnesium. "These capitalists are like leeches who suck the blood out of the factory worker," Sumi, Mihwa and I would recite to each other during break times.

One night, my mother was late getting home from school. I cooked the wheat rice for our family and served kimchi. We ate in silence, even Hyungchul and Sunyoung, who usually fought with each other over who had the largest portion.

When my mother got home, Sunyoung and I were in our long johns, brushing our teeth.

"Let me show you something," Umma said, pulling the two of us into the main room. She carefully shut the door to my father's room, where he stood as usual at his table drawing a new boat. Then my mother sang a song for us as she glided around

80

the room, her thin arms waving in the air like butterfly wings.

On her third twirl around the room, she whisked me into her arms to show me how the dance went. I giggled. It felt like we were back at my grandparents' farm in Hoeryong. Just as my mother let go of my arms to take Sunyoung's, my father threw open the door to his room. It banged against the wall, toppling some dishes that crashed into pieces when they hit the floor.

My mother stopped abruptly, her skirt billowing out around her. Abuji's face was red, and his chest was puffed out just like the military *ajussi* we saw marching on the streets.

"Did you stay late at work to dance?" he bellowed, making me jump.

Umma stood still. "Yes," she said, lowering her head. "We are practicing a song to sing at the concert."

"I've told you my opinion. A woman can only get into trouble by being involved in the arts. I forbid you to continue. Do you understand? No more singing teams at work!"

Still in a rage, my father grabbed the broom and started hitting my mother across the back of her legs. Sunyoung and I ran to join Hyungchul and Hyungwoo in the room in which we slept. They had already pulled the duvet up so only their eyes showed. As Sunyoung and I huddled in the corner, she clamped her hands over her ears. I listened to the broom handle smack hard against my mother's skin.

Eventually, I closed my eyes. Now I knew why my mother never liked for me to sing.

"What is a nobleman?" I whispered to myself, the question the flower girl had asked her mother.

"If only such a man were to appear to you, as if in a fairy tale," I replied, whispering the mother's answer.

Chapter Nine

DURING THE PLANTING and harvesting seasons, the fourth and fifth months and the ninth and tenth months of each year, students in the higher grades were assigned to farms in the countryside. We had to move there, either living with a family or being billeted in government-run compounds. Once I was sent to the same farm as my close friends Mihwa and Sumi, but the other times I was assigned to farms far away, where there was no one I knew.

The first year I did this farm duty, I expected I would at least be well fed. I was shocked to discover I was rationed even less food there, despite all the hard work I was doing, than I got when I attended school. I received a bowl of wheat rice for breakfast, and sometimes the cook gave me some cabbage. That was all I had to sustain myself on until evening, when I was given the same meal again.

That first year, I was so hungry that I would tuck corn and turnip into my pockets as I left the field. I got away with it for a few days. But then the guards watching over the workers caught on. A female guard patted me down and discovered the stolen items. She took them from me and started yelling that being a thief was being disloyal to the ideals of our great leader. My eyes grew misty, which I hoped the guard would perceive as tears, my repentance for stealing. But the truth was, I was sad because I was starving and no longer had the extra food. As I walked back to the home of the family that was billeting me, I strategized about ways to steal food in the future, including hiding the vegetables in my underwear. That would be far more difficult than to slip something discreetly into my pockets, though, since the workers were always watching one another. I ended up just going hungry.

DURING MY SECOND-LAST year of *Joong-hak-kyo,* or middle school, Grade 9, I was sent to a farm on the Tumen River for the harvesting season. The air was fresh with the scent of grass but also something I had never smelled before: fish from the river.

That year, to our surprise, Mihwa and I were billeted with the same family. Within a few days of arriving, the two of us began to steal food. In the mornings, when the aging mother of the family, her daughter and her daughters-in-law headed to the river to wash the men's shirts and pants, we pretended to follow the men in the family as they left for the fields. But as soon as they disappeared over the hills, Mihwa and I would duck behind the house and sneak up on the cage where the chickens were kept.

We would wait patiently until one of the chickens made some clucking sounds and an egg popped out. Then we would snatch the egg, poke a hole in the end of it with a stick, and take turns drinking the contents. We managed this every morning for an entire month, until we greedily started taking an egg each. One morning after that, instead of us outwitting the family, the male head outwitted us.

Just as I had finished slurping my egg and was licking my lips, the man came up behind me and began beating the backs of my legs with a stick. He used so much force that the fabric on my pants tore and blood was drawn. He did the same to Mihwa. By the time he was finished, we could barely walk and were wincing with pain. But we were not allowed to wash or bandage our wounds. We limped our way across the hills to work the fields.

From that day on, no one in the family spoke to us. The mother would push our rice and turnip across to us in the mornings, but our portions were cut in half as further punishment for our crime. What had started as the best work placement of my school years turned into the worst. My eyes clouded over from hunger, and my body grew weak. My nails and hair began to break. My moods slipped into melancholy.

Mihwa and I were not allowed to bathe in the house, so we went to the river. I did not venture far into the icy waters, barely wading in past my knees before crouching in the waves to wash my body with a rag. For one thing, I didn't know how to swim. For another, the river was on the border between our country and China. I watched people who lived in the area swim right out in the river and say hello to the Chinese people who lived on the other side. "Leave the Chinese pigs alone," I wanted to scream at the family who had punished me for eating eggs. I felt what they were doing, in speaking to the Chinese was far worse than my own crime.

"There is nothing worse than befriending Chinese *daenum* or Russian *mawoojae*," I whispered to Mihwa.

Mihwa and I had seen Russians before. Like the Chinese, they came to Yuseon to sell items like cigarettes and rice. Russians had white, white skin, blue eyes, and bodies twice if not three times the size of ours. They wore big billowy coats and furry hats in winter.

"Chinese and Russians will try to kidnap us," Mihwa whispered back. "Only we North Koreans are pure of spirit and mind. All the rest of the people are beasts."

That night, neither Mihwa nor I could sleep. My mind raced with all the bad things the Chinese men on the other side could do to us, including crossing to our side, breaking the windows, stealing the pots and pans, and then tossing Mihwa and me over their shoulders and smuggling us into China, where we would never see our families again.

In the days that followed, these thoughts became so loud inside my head that I worried my fears might be heard by others. I wanted to get as far away from the river as I could. I felt sick to my stomach to see the family we were billeted with up close, knowing they had been talking with the Chinese earlier in the day. Mihwa and I spent our days working in silence, our eyes red from lack of sleep and our skin yellowing from malnutrition. The only thing that soothed us were the calls of owls in the middle of the night, trying to sing us to sleep. When we heard them, we would reach out and hold each other's hands.

THAT YEAR WHEN we returned to school, there was a new girl in our class: Youngsook, whom I nicknamed Pumpkin for two reasons. For one, she was very fat. The folds of her stomach bulged over the belt on her skirt. Also, her family grew many vegetables in their yard, including pumpkins. Pumpkin's family had taken over Daechul's house after the Boweebu removed all of the previous family's belongings, including photographs.

The pumpkin vines and the fences surrounding the house made it look like a fortress. "I heard that Daechul's mother was sending messages to the south on a radio from the mountains," I told Pumpkin and her mother one afternoon when Sumi and I were there visiting.

"How do you feel living in a home once lived in by spies?" Sumi asked them.

Pumpkin's mother declared firmly that she and her husband were Party members. When her mother left the house to hang some laundry, Pumpkin whispered to Sumi and me: "A girl in school is dating a married man. They're having an affair."

I stood frozen in shock. "What does this have to do with your house and spies?" I asked finally collecting myself.

"Oh, that." Pumpkin waved her hand. "This is more important. This student is unmarried and the man is married. It is very scandalous."

I frowned. "Have you ever checked the walls of your home?" I asked, trying to change the subject. "Maybe the family left notes tucked in hiding places, chronicling their activities."

"Don't be silly." Pumpkin waved her hand again. "You must understand how dangerous it is for the girl to be doing this with that man."

"Well, why don't they stop?" Sumi said, caught up in the story.

"You can't just stop when you are in love," Pumpkin sighed, clasping her hands to her heart. "Love is not something that you go out and get and then turn off when the mind says it's not right. Love settles in the heart like a butterfly, and it must be treated delicately, allowed to leave or stay as it wishes. People do wicked things to each other when they hold on too tight. They can do things in the name of love that hurt other people."

I didn't really understand what Pumpkin told Sumi and me that day. I was more interested in spies and our safety and in our allegiance to the great father. Besides, love to me was a sinking feeling, not taking off like butterflies. Sinking like one of my father's ships. I had no idea then that my feelings might change.

CHULNAHM WAS A boy in the same grade as me. Both his parents were members of the Party, and his father was a supervisor in a manufacturing company that made wood and iron products. Chulnahm had broad shoulders and eyes that, when the sun hit them a certain way, appeared amber, just like my own. He had strong legs and a crooked smile.

When we were still children but after I had started school, Chulnahm and I had sometimes met on the hill near our houses and tobogganed together in the winter. I would wrap my arms tightly around his stomach, my chest against his back, as we slid down the hill on a wooden toboggan his father had made for Chulnahm and his older brothers. Since we lived in the same grouping of houses, we walked home from school together and we often got together to do our homework and study. We would sit beside each other and engage in elbow wars until we finally settled down and focused on our work. After we had completed our assignments, Chulnahm would lean back against the wall with one knee pulled up and listen as I read him some of my original writings. I thought nothing of our friendship until I was sixteen and found myself sinking one afternoon when he said goodbye.

"Big sister says that when lovers meet, they walk side by side, their arms swinging in unison, their steps matching each other's," Pumpkin informed me one day at break-time. I'd given in. All she talked about was affairs and lovers. For us to remain friends, I had to follow along.

"But a man proposes to a woman by first spending time with her family," I replied. "Love comes after everyone agrees."

"You think so?" Pumpkin smiled, her fat cheeks scrunching up into balls, her eyes narrowing so much I could barely see her pupils. "Big sister says people who are in love don't sit across from each other but side by side. They become one. Kind of like you and Chulnahm," she smirked, tilting her head to the side.

I gasped.

"Yes," Sumi chimed in. "When I see you two walking home from school, from the side I can't tell you are two people. You walk as if you are one."

"You look like apricot trees," Pumpkin teased, "standing in a perfect line."

I stepped back and shook my head. "How can you say such a thing! I am just a young girl," I stammered, "and he is a friend. Never, never, would I do such a thing. I will marry when my mother and father choose my match."

Pumpkin and Sumi laughed as I stood before them, my face burning.

FOR WEEKS AFTERWARDS, I avoided walking home from school with Chulnahm, darting out the back of the building even though he waited for me out front.

As I half-ran, half-walked up the streets toward my home, two voices warred inside my head.

"We grew up with each other," I heard myself say. "His father is a vice-supervisor in a government factory and his mother oversees a government-run restaurant. We would be seen as a good match. I might finally make my grandmother proud of me, by marrying such a man. She might even give me a candy."

But the reality was far different. "I'm only sixteen. I won't ever be a member of the Party. Chulnahm will never marry me. He will join the military and meet someone his family will accept." In the end, these realistic thoughts won. I knew the most I could aspire to was to become a kindergarten teacher like my mother. Even for that, my marks at school might not be high enough. I vowed never to think of the other feelings I had for Chulnahm again.

I did start to walk home from school with him again though, firmly believing that we were just friends. "There will never be anything between us," I had assured Pumpkin and Sumi. Yet, occasionally, as we walked, I would look down and see that Chulnahm and I were walking in tandem, our arms and legs moving at exactly the same rate. Whenever I noticed this, I would speed up or slow down, so that our steps no longer matched.

Chapter Ten

MY MOTHER'S HAND shook as she looked through my final marks. "How did this happen?" she eventually exclaimed, looking at me with angry eyes.

I shook my head as I crumpled to the floor in dismay. My marks were average, not good enough for me to gain admittance to university.

"I didn't study hard enough," I stammered. "I wanted to. I tried. Now I can't be a teacher like you."

"No," my mother replied curtly. "You'll have to become a factory worker instead."

"I didn't mean for this to happen," I said, my eyes fixed on the floor. "I just couldn't wake in the mornings. I was always tired and hungry. I am not like Sunyoung, who works hours upon hours, studying all of her coursework. I just wanted to write poems and stories."

"You'll have your own children one day," my mother said, moving toward the door to my father's office. "You can teach them what you hoped to teach as a kindergarten instructor. But now, you must tell your father the news. You will start technical school, *Yunhapgisoolyang sung bahn*, for mechanical skills training in a few months."

MY FATHER WAS not pleased I had done so poorly at school. But he didn't beat me, which I had expected him to do. Instead, he ignored me in the months that followed. The day I was due to start technical school, my father left for work early. I didn't even see him that morning. But I did see Chulnahm.

I was surprised when we bumped into one another at the train station, for I was certain Chulnahm had gone off to the military. All young men did when they finished school. "I'm taking another year before I join," he explained, anticipating my question. "I'm going to Yunhapgisoolyang sung bahn where I'm going to learn to weld."

And so our friendship resumed, as did our walking side by side in unison. I no longer looked down to check. I liked feeling Chulnahm beside me. Now I thought of nothing else when I was with him.

Some of the girls at my new school were dating already, and they spoke openly about the young men they met after classes or in the evenings, sneaking out to see them when their fathers were not home. When I overheard their whispered conversations about kissing these men I forced my attention back to my lessons. I was learning how to use heavy machines. I would marry and kiss my husband when my mother said I was ready, not before, I lectured myself.

Other than Chulnahm, I spoke to none of the boys at the technical school. I would lower my head whenever a male student walked past me in the hallways. Only one young man, Ilhyun, seemed to notice me. He was slim with lithe arm movements and a quick smile I did not trust. He would wink at me when we passed on the grounds at school. A few times that autumn, Ilhyun ran after me when I went home at midday to finish the bowl of rice I had saved from the morning. Pretending I did not see him, I ran faster to stay ahead.

In a month when the frost was still on the ground by mid-morning, my mother presented me with a new outfit: green pants and a matching jacket. I was proud of the green pantsuit, and I felt grown up as I set off for school.

When Ilhyun saw me coming out of the women's classroom later that day, he stopped and stared, a big grin crossing his face. I lowered my head to avoid his eyes, quickening my pace as I headed for the women's washroom. I opened the washroom door and then quickly slammed it shut, leaning against the door as Ilhyun pushed on the other side, trying to get in. He banged his fists against the wood and pleaded for me to come out.

Finally there was silence. When I put my ear to the door and listened, I could hear Ilhyun pacing back and forth. I couldn't remain in the washroom forever so I decided I would try to skirt past Ilhyun and get back to my classroom.

I opened the door a crack, then slipped out. As Ilhyun turned and saw me, I stopped in mid-stride, paralyzed on the spot. The veins on Ilhyun's forehead were throbbing. "Why do you run away?" he asked sharply, stepping so close our bodies nearly touched.

I lowered my eyes to the floor, feeling Ilhyun's heavy breathing on my cheek. My body had started to tremble.

"What are you doing?" I heard Chulnahm call out. I looked up and saw him coming toward us at the same moment Ilhyun touched my hand lightly. "I like you," Ilhyun said near my ear.

"You stupid girl," Chulnahm chided, reaching us and pushing Ilhyun away. "Go to your classroom."

I darted past them, not daring to look back. Chulnahm's words stung as if I had been slapped in the face. From that day on, I refused to walk with him again.

THE YEAR BEFORE I graduated from high school, my paternal grandfather had come to live with us for a few months. My grandmother had died a year earlier, and he was lonely.

My grandfather shuffled from room to room. He got my name and the names of my siblings mixed up. He ate double his ration of food, meaning the rest of us had less. My mother had stopped working a few years earlier to be home when my sister and brothers got back from school. The little money my parents had saved was reserved for Sunyoung's and my own wedding and dowries so there was none left over for extra food.

One afternoon during his stay, my grandfather had asked to speak with my mother alone. He pulled her into my father's room and shut the door. Curious, I put my ear against the wall and listened.

"The foundations of this family are not good," I heard him say, his voice deep but shaky in his old age. "Your family is full of South Korean defectors. Because of that, my son has suffered. He should have been made supervisor at the factory years ago. He is still a labourer, and that is because of you."

"He just received news that he will be given a promotion to *bujikjangjang*, vice-manager," I heard my mother reply.

"That is nothing!" my grandfather exclaimed, the wall shaking as his fist pounded against it on the other side. "All my other children have high positions in the Party. Changwoon, my first-born son, has the least. You are the downfall of this family."

When I heard my grandfather shuffle toward the door, I moved away quickly and pretended to be doing my homework. My mother came out of the room shortly after, her face red from embarrassment and tears. She looked at me and sighed. She knew I had overheard.

Since then, I had accepted that I would never get Party membership. I knew there was no point in my even attempting to do so. I would not be able to find a sponsor to guarantee my good standing in society so my marriage prospects were limited. When my paternal grandfather died later that year, part of me was happy. He would no longer have to see what a failure his eldest son's family had become.

A few months after the incident with Ilhyun, Chulnahm started coming to my family's house after school. He would talk with my mother and offer to help her with the farming. I would watch from the window as they dug up the earth and watered the plants. When Chulnahm came into the house for some water one afternoon, I rushed past him not stopping until I was outdoors.

"What is going on with you two?" my mother demanded.

I shrugged my shoulders and remained silent.

Over the last few months of school, Chulnahm would seek me out after class and try to strike up a conversation. I ignored him.

"You know he is courting you," my mother told me one evening after Chulnahm had visited, this time helping her put down basins in the house since the roof leaked. "If you want to proceed with this, you will need to visit with his mother and family next."

"No," I replied, stomping my foot. I replaced one of the basins Chulnahm had laid down with a bigger one, rolling my eyes at my mother. I was still too angry at Chulnahm to even consider it.

THAT AUTUMN, I started work at a metal manufacturing factory, overseeing the compression machine. I travelled to work with my father on the train, since my factory was located just a few blocks from his. I buried any thoughts I had of Chulnahm. Every time his face popped into my mind, I would shake the image away. He had joined the military by now, so it was easy. I no longer saw him.

But as harvesting season arrived, the cloak of anger I had put up toward Chulnahm had disappeared, and in its place was longing. My daydreams were full of Chulnahm's laugh, his smile, and the way we had walked side by side, as if we were one. At work, I could not focus properly on operating the machine. I was always in a fog, thinking of Chulnahm.

Finally I came to the conclusion that I had to reach him. I had to tell him. I had to let him know.

I wanted to be his wife.

Chapter Eleven

I SENT A note to the army barracks where Chulnahm's mother told me he was stationed.

> Dear Chulnahm,
>   I will wait for you until you come back. If you don't want me to wait, tell me, and I won't. Can you give me a response?
>   Sunhwa

After that, I waited. I worked alternating shifts at my job. One week I would start at 8 a.m. and work until 4 p.m. The following week, I worked from 4 p.m. until midnight. The week after that, I would work the night shift, from midnight until 8 a.m. Every Saturday morning, I took part in the total life retrospective with my co-workers.

The factory where I worked removed impure materials from metals mined in other places of the country. I was soon put in charge of depositing the waste materials on a conveyer belt, which took the substances to a truck. The truck disposed of the garbage in an open valley in a rural area.

As I performed my duties, I imagined what Chulnahm would

look like in his pressed green military uniform. I envisioned his sleek black hair, picturing him as he learned to use guns to fight our enemies. During work breaks, I would close my eyes and think of Chulnahm as my saviour, like the flower girl's brother. Chulnahm would protect me from the Chinese on the other side of the river and the Russians with their rough language that sounded like dogs barking. He would protect me from the capitalists and landlords in the south, who were disloyal to our great father.

When months passed and I heard nothing from him, my heart grew heavy. One day I confided in some of the older women who worked in the factory with me. Unni, a woman with wide swaying hips who reminded me of Pumpkin, wagged her finger and berated me for not coming to her sooner. "I would have told you to send the letter to his residential complex, not the barracks," she scolded. "I'm sure he never got it."

"Sister, what should I do?" I asked her. "Should I write him again?"

"I don't think he got it," interjected a petite woman whose first baby was nursing at her breast. While the woman worked, her baby remained in the nursery. "Yes, you need to write again. But this time do as Unni says. Mail it directly to your man."

Unni sighed. "Don't be foolish. It is too late. He's moved on. You had your chance. He's going to be in the army now for ten years. He'll find someone near where he is stationed, someone less difficult."

"No!" I cried out in sorrow.

"Don't worry," Unni said. "You will have other prospects. You just need to, hmm . . . " She ran her eyes up and down my body. "Can you come to my house on Sunday?"

THAT WEEKEND, UNNI plopped me down on some plastic sheets in the kitchen of her home. She put my hair in curlers and squeezed some chemicals from a bottle over my head. "Once I fix you up," she said as she kneaded my scalp, "you'll get another man." While I waited for my hair to set, she showed me how to put on white powder and red lipstick. I let Unni do whatever she wanted, wishing that Chulnahm would be able to see me.

But when she was finished and I looked at myself in a cracked mirror, I shuddered. My hair was not curly but frizzy, like the feathers of a dead sparrow. My face didn't look grown-up and beautiful, but rather like a painting done by a child unable to colour in between the lines. I was so dismayed, I wrapped a towel around my head for the walk home. As soon as I arrived, I ducked into the outhouse and used the cold water in the pail to scrub my face with soap. I then snuck into the pantry and tried to flatten my hair using sesame oil.

After several more months had passed, my manager approached me to take a job in the country. A tunnel was being drilled through a mountain near the coast for use as a military base if the south invaded, and I would be helping operate the drilling machines.

"Is anyone else coming from the factory?" I asked him.

"No, just you. They are all mothers. They cannot leave their babies."

"How long will I be gone?" I asked.

"As long as a year," he said.

One word stood out in my mind from our conversation: "military." I washed my hair four times to get the oil out and curled it with rags in an attempt to remove the frizz. I put white powder on my cheeks and started dabbing red lipstick on my lips every morning, at midday and again in the evening. If Chulnahm was not going to be a part of my life, then I would find another military man at the mountain who would marry me. When Chulnahm learned of that, it would be his punishment.

ABOUT FORTY PEOPLE from different factories across Chosun met at the coast. There were only five women, and we slept together in the small wooden house built nearest the urinals. I started work the day after arriving, overseeing the machines that were digging out the mountain. Whenever I could, I would look out at the green sea with its frothy waves and winds that tossed my curls. The ocean stretched to the east as far as my eyes could strain. I imagined one of my father's ships coming over the horizon. He hadn't even said goodbye. My mother had been stern, as if she knew the real reason behind my excitement at leaving. "Don't meet a boy," she had warned me. "You'll get pregnant. Just keep to yourself. Do your job, and when you return, your father and I will find you a husband."

But I didn't want their husband, unless it was Chulnahm. I vowed to find one myself over the course of the year. And I did. Myungin was tall, with broad shoulders, and a toothy smile like the men in the magazines my father hid in his chest and forbade me to read. His black eyes sparkled when he looked at me. Of course, I looked down when that happened. But as I did, in my mind's eye I saw the two of us walking in tandem.

Every morning as we rose in our house to get ready before the morning meal, Myungin would walk past the women's dormitory and knock. I would rush wide-eyed to the door. By the time I flung it open, he had left. I could see only his back as he made his way to the cafeteria. But I breathed in his scent, which floated in the air: a scent of soap and manly sweat, since he was a labourer, mixed with sea salt and fresh green grass. I knew a man must approach the woman first, so I dared not speak to him. At first, I didn't even know his name or whether or not he already had a wife.

Every morning after his knock, I changed quickly into my work outfit, dabbed some powder on my face, applied lipstick and smoothed down my hair, which was made more frizzy than ever by the humid air so close to the sea. I would then get my shaking body over to the cafeteria and sit at the back, at a table facing his.

"His name is Myungin," said one of my co-workers one morning. She was a middle-aged woman whose eldest son and his wife had just had a son of their own, making her a proud halmuni. That evening, just before we went to bed, the woman had some exciting news. "Myungin has asked me to accompany you to breakfast tomorrow," she explained as my heart began to beat wildly. "He wants you to sit beside him."

"Chulnahm," I mused as I dozed off that night, "I don't even know what I liked about you. Now I have Myungin."

At breakfast the next morning, Myungin held a chair out for me to sit, his eyes dancing. He reminded me of a movie star, his muscles flexing under his khaki work shirt, his movements liquid and full of confidence. He asked me simple questions, including my name, hometown and age.

"Tell me about your family?" he asked. I twirled my rice in the tin bowl with my chopstick, unable to eat, unable to think, unable to feel anything except an electricity blowing through me like the sea winds outside. When Myungin smiled, his front left tooth, capped in gold, twinkled in the morning light.

In the weeks that followed, we ate our meals together morning and night, saying little to each other as our bodies moved in unison. One day, my new manager announced that I was being promoted. I would now be on the same team as Myungin, overseeing a different group of labourers. "We believe that a single woman and a single man working together will make each of you work harder," the manager said, "to show each other what good comrades you are."

"So he is single," I thought, sighing.

Sometimes at night, one of the women in my bunker would turn on the radio. There was a Russian song that often was played in between Chunbok and Manghil. After we'd been working together for a few weeks, Myungin sang me a line from that same song: "I do not love you, I adore you . . . "

"Sister," I asked the woman with the radio that evening. "What does *adore* mean?"

"It means love," she smiled.

"And what does love mean?" I asked.

"What you are feeling for Myungin."

ON A SNOWY day in the first month of the new year, my foot got stuck under a cart carrying some rocks. Myungin, who was by my side, yelled for help, then lifted the heavy cart off my foot. He slipped off my shoe, and while we waited for a stretcher, he cradled my injured foot in his hands. When no assistance came, he finally swung me onto his broad back and carried me down the mountain to the health clinic. He paced outside the window as the nurse bandaged my foot, then carried me to the wooden house where I slept. He tucked me in and left before anyone saw him, since men were forbidden entry to our quarters. I still knew little about this man, other than that his strength made me feel weak. When my foot was healed and winter had fled to make room for planting season, Myungin and I began walking hand in hand in the fields, watching the sun rise in the early morning and set in the evenings. I didn't think any longer about my plan to find a husband or to punish Chulnahm. I was simply in love.

Our work term in the mountain ended that autumn on a dark day when rain created waves in the gutter. I ate my last meal sitting beside Myungin and we sat side by side on the train in silence as we returned to our homes.

My stop was first, and I knew my mother was waiting. As I got up to go, Myungin pulled me quickly into his arms and whispered, "I adore you. Come to my train station in two days. I will wait for you."

He slipped a piece of paper into my pocket. The name of his train station and a time to meet were written on it; I couldn't help but be struck that the words I had sent to Chulnahm, Myungin now said to me.

Two days later, on an evening so still you could hear the owls hoot, I told my mother I had to go to a meeting at my factory. Instead, I made my way to the train station. I was wearing my only dress, which I had bought with the savings from my job. It was navy blue with tiny black dots on the smooth, silky fabric, and it drew in at the waist, shaping my figure into an hourglass. My face was white, the powder perfectly smooth and blended. My lips felt plump and full under the lipstick I had applied.

"I adore you," Myungin said again when I disembarked from the train to find him on the platform. We walked without many words to his parents' house, where the first thing he did was give me a bowl of sugar: a sign of his intent to marry me.

Myungin's father had worked in Pyongyang, he told me, and that is why his mother could serve me candy powder and *bbang*, the special Korean sweet bread—pricey items rationed for the elite. For our meal, we had potatoes instead of rice. Myungin's mother explained that her husband owned a company that sold clothes and furniture the Chinese left behind when they came to Chosun to sell their wares.

"A petty salesman," I said confidently, wanting to impress her with my knowledge. Instead of praising, though, she became defensive.

"No. He distributes the items to markets in the bigger cities. We are Party members," she said, as Myungin and his father nodded proudly.

I had heard that only people who had lost their positions in the Party departed the city. All of the older people I knew had harboured dreams at one point in their lives of doing so well that the Party would ask them to move to Pyongyang. It never was the other way around. No one ever wanted to leave. But I didn't ask Myungin's mother or father about that.

A month and a half later, Myungin sent a message through a friend to my factory, where I was back at my old job. This time I ate a meal of noodles with turnip with his mother while the men smoked cigarettes outside. She asked me questions about my family, starting with my father. I explained that he was the vice-manager of a factory and a Party member. She smiled, pleased with my answer. I trembled as we spoke, terrified she would ask about my mother. But just then, the men returned. Would I come with him now to visit his sister, who lived a few houses away, Myungin asked.

That was it. My palms started to perspire. Myungin was going to ask me to marry him.

Chapter Twelve

AS WE ENTERED his sister's small home, the warmth from the fire in the kitchen hit my cheeks, making me blush. Myungin's brother-in-law was sitting cross-legged on the floor drinking *nongtaegi*, a popular alcohol. Myungin motioned for me to sit, too, explaining that his sister was visiting some friends but would be back soon.

The brother-in-law spoke for a while about his job in the factory, then stood up and said he'd go get his wife. After he left, Myungin pulled a guitar from one of the cupboards and began playing the Russian song I had heard on the radio. My body swayed as he sang the lyrics. I closed my eyes dreamily, but when I opened them, I saw that Myungin had inched his way toward me, his feet nearly touching my own. I pulled my legs away, my heart racing. He moved closer, then put down the guitar and started hugging me.

I leapt up and stammered that I had to go to the outhouse. But when I tried the doors, they were locked. I turned toward Myungin and, in a quavering voice, asked him to let me leave.

"After," he said, taking my arm.

I pulled myself loose and yanked on the doorknob. It wouldn't budge, so I raced to the other door and banged on it. I did this over and over again, Myungin grinning the entire time. Finally, exhausted, I gave in and sat down. Myungin moved in behind me and started unbuttoning my cotton shirt.

"No," I said, barely audible. "I . . . I . . . could get pregnant." I closed my eyes, knowing I was trapped. "I have never been with a man before," I lamented.

I didn't struggle or cry out as I felt Myungin on top of me and then inside me, his scent of perspiration, soap and breath that smelled of powder candy making me choke.

I was in a daze as Myungin walked me to the train station. He didn't squeeze my hand like he usually did when I stepped away from him and onto the train. For my part, I didn't turn to wave. I sank into the vinyl seat and drifted into a thick fog, exhausted by the heavy burden of knowing someone I trusted had betrayed me.

AFTER THAT NIGHT, I didn't hear anything from Myungin for weeks. I didn't dare tell my mother what had happened. She had predicted this, after all. I became aloof, somber and quiet. I hid myself away, coming out only when I had to work. Then when my shifts were finished, I disappeared again, too ashamed to face my life. I told everyone who asked that I was not feeling well.

After three months had passed, I set off for the factory where Myungin worked. I waited outside the building until his shift ended. As I saw him come toward me, lighting up a cigarette, I shivered. He looked different, his body hard, his eyes cold. When he walked right past me as if I were a stranger, I followed him.

"Why are you avoiding me?" I called out at one point. He stopped and turned.

"You lied to me," he said in a low voice, so his colleagues

heading to the train wouldn't hear. "You teased me. You forced me to do those things to you." He spat, then took a long drag on his cigarette. Blowing smoke into the air, he rolled his eyes at me. "You said you had never been with a man before. You lied. You are not a virgin."

For a moment, I was speechless. "Why would you say this?" I finally managed to get out.

He stepped toward me so swiftly I worried he was about to knock me over. "When we were up on the mountain, there were soldiers guarding us," he hissed. "I saw you talking to them. Your co-workers saw you talking to them. You were with one of them." He stomped his cigarette out on the pavement with his black boot and walked away.

I swallowed my tears as I rode back on the train. For the rest of the week, I couldn't eat. I couldn't sleep. I tossed and turned on the mat where I lay. I told my mother I was sick with the flu. Somehow I had to reach Myungin. I had to speak to him, get him to listen.

The following Sunday, curled up on my sleeping mat, I wrote Myungin a letter, using my father's fountain pen. "Why do you listen to other people? I am a virgin, or I was. I adore you," I ended the letter.

Just as I had folded the paper into three, my mother walked up behind me and grabbed it. I looked at her fearfully as she read.

"Who is this man?" she demanded. I started sobbing, hiding my face in the duvet. "Who is he?" she shouted again. I was crying too hard to answer.

When my father came home that night, my mother showed him the letter. He frowned as he read, his brow pinched, his nostrils flared. When he was finished, he ordered me to tell him everything about Myungin.

WHEN I RETURNED from work the next day, my parents were waiting. My father had left work early, something he seldom did. I lowered my head to avoid their eyes.

"I went to Myungin's factory today," my mother began.

I started to shake, fearing what was to come.

"I met with the Party secretary at his office. Sunhwa, do you know anything about this man, Myungin?" my mother continued.

I remained silent.

"Do you know anything?" my father repeated angrily, slapping his thigh with his hand.

"No," I said under my breath.

"He has been in prison," my mother said.

"A year," my father added. "He spent a year in prison."

I looked up and searched their faces. I could see they were telling the truth and I was horrified. "What for?" I stammered.

"His father held a high position in the foreign currency division in Pyongyang," my father said. "The Party secretary would not tell your mother what, but the father did something wrong, and the entire family was sent away. The father and Myungin had to work in the construction unit. While there, Myungin got drunk on nongtaegi and beat up a co-worker. The man he beat up was a *chomoseng*, a good person. He was from a very good family, well respected in the Party. Myungin was sent to jail, where he had to do hard labour. When you met him on the mountain, he had just finished his prison term."

I stood speechless, my stomach churning.

"You're never to see him again," my mother ordered.

My father exploded when I did not reply. "Did you hear?"

"Yes," I whispered. The house was filled with the silence of my broken dreams. "I understand. I won't ever see him again."

MY PARENTS' WRATH did little to heal my broken heart. Worse, I soon realized that I was pregnant. I was terrified, and I didn't know what to do.

For the next few weeks, I did very little other than work at the factory and help my mother cook and tend to the farm. We occasionally watched a film together. One evening, I went alone to a repeat showing of *The Flower Girl*. As I walked home, singing the flower girl's songs to myself, Myungin approached suddenly out of the darkness. For a moment, we stared at each other. I could not move. My body shook with fear.

He fell to his knees and buried his face in his hands. "I am so sorry," he sobbed. "I was such a fool to believe those things about you. I was wrong. You are a good person, and I am bad."

I had imagined this apology many times, and I bit my trembling lip to conceal my tears. "My family won't let me see you ever again," I said with as much confidence as I could muster. The truth, though, was that I wanted to see this man. I wanted him to hold me. I wanted him to tell me I would be safe.

The light from the full moon lit Myungin's face. "If you can forgive me, I promise to never make you cry again. I am sorry," he continued as I stared at this man, whose face had haunted my dreams. "Please, please, please forgive me."

I swallowed hard, my throat dry and sore.

Myungin and I talked until the morning sun cast a dull light on the field where we sat together. Myungin explained about his past and his family and told me how he had turned his life around. He had a stable job in the factory and he wanted a family. He said he wanted me. He begged me for a second chance, even when I whispered to him that I was pregnant.

As I rose to go home, hoping to slip into bed before my parents woke, I agreed to marry Myungin.

What I dared not tell him was that I wasn't sure what would be worse: being an unwed woman raising a child alone, or being married to him. I picked what I believed to be the lesser of two evils.

Chapter Thirteen

I WAS TWENTY-TWO when I married Myungin. Snow fell on my wedding day, the twenty-fourth day of the last month of 1990. That should have been an omen for me; couples never wed at that time of year. But I refused to listen to my father's laments that day, as I had earlier. "Why does Myungin want to be married so fast? I do not understand what he is up to," he fretted, pacing the room as my mother pinned an apricot flower made of pink paper on to the bun she had made of my hair.

It was true that Myungin had chosen the day but I hadn't complained. At least this way I wouldn't have to tell my parents about my pregnancy. When the child was born, I would tell them the baby was conceived on our wedding night and arrived early. I wasn't showing yet, even though four months had passed. I just looked as if I'd been eating a bit more.

"I will ask my brother to see what is going on when he takes you to Myungin's house," my father continued. "I don't approve of this wedding."

"Stop," my mother hissed. "It is done now. Let her have a happy day."

My father and brothers left the room as my mother helped me dress in a pink traditional skirt and top. She had spent nearly half of our family's savings on fabric for the outfit. As she admired my appearance, my relatives started to arrive, including my aunt Youngrahn, who was festively made up for the occasion. She had outlined her lips in a darker shade of red than her lipstick and powdered her face perfectly white.

Soon one of my father's brothers showed up with two chickens. Chickens were hard to find and expensive to buy, but very auspicious. My mother cleaned and boiled the birds and then placed them on the table, surrounded by trays of candies made into miniature pagodas and flowers, including a pink lotus with yellow stamens and green leaves. My father and uncle pierced the chickens with sticks so they would sit upright, stuck red chili peppers in their mouth and arranged them facing each other in the traditional way. One chicken, however, kept slumping forward.

"This is not a good sign for a long life of happiness," Youngrahn scowled. "When the chickens look alive, it means the bride and groom will be in love forever. When one chicken can't do what it is meant to do, it means one member of the couple is not sincere."

Her words frightened me, and I started to perspire, fearful that Myungin would cancel the ceremony. I wrung my hands as we waited for him to arrive with his father and brothers.

When I heard the knock on the door, I nearly leapt out of my pink slippers. "Don't move," my mother ordered, as my father and uncle let them in. "A wife must always follow their husband. You should let Myungin lead you. Once you move into his home, you will become the *myuneuri*, the daughter-in-law of the family. You must listen to your husband and all of his family."

I snuck a look at Myungin in his black suit and white shirt as he took a seat at the head of the table bearing the chicken and the sweets. His brothers sat one to each side. In the traditional way, Myungin was supposed to point to the foods he wanted packed and taken to his house as gifts for his parents. He asked only for the chickens, though, which I didn't like. Of all the food that filled the table he picked the chickens that had kept falling forward. It felt like a further bad omen. My mother had spent money from our meager savings to prepare the table of candies and sweets, in anticipation that most of the food would be taken to Myungin's family as a sign of respect and good fortune. Now her eyes were red as she held back her tears. She too, I felt, saw his only picking the chickens as a very bad sign.

My mother served Myungin and the other men a meal of white rice with three boiled eggs, blood sausages, squid and *samhynagsoo*, a special liquor that had been given to us on the birthday of the great leader, Kim Il-sung, and saved for this occasion. I left the room so the men could eat alone. When Myungin was done, I knew he would twist the neck of one of the chickens. When that happened, my mother beckoned for me to return. She packed up the poultry into a small box for Myungin to take to his mother. Myungin and his father and brother left soon after. My brothers loaded the *hahm*, a wedding chest of dishes, chopsticks, linens, towels and bedding, on top of a car borrowed from my father's factory, securing it to the roof with heavy rope.

By the time I arrived at Myungin's parents' house with my uncle and aunt as escorts, the light snowfall had turned into a blizzard. Myungin's house wasn't much warmer than the temperature outside, and because the electricity had gone out, the rooms were lit with kerosene lamps. Everything was going wrong. "Where is the rope that will lead me to the sky?" I asked myself as Myungin's family greeted my uncle and aunt.

My relatives handed Myungin's father the rest of the money my parents were contributing to our new life together.

I took my seat at a small table off to the side, with my aunt to the left of me. The table was completely covered by a tower made of candies. Myungin and his family sat at a large table close by. I gasped when I noticed the chickens in the centre of it. "Those are my mother's chickens," I protested silently, fighting the urge to cover my mouth in horror. My uncle's gaze was fixed on the chickens as well, and I could see from the lines on his forehead that he was in shock. Nothing could be a greater sign of disrespect to my family than for Myungin's family to reuse the chickens.

Myungin's mother served bowls of white rice with three eggs on top to those seated at the main table. Myungin, smirking, leaned over to speak to me. "Your family's food was all looks and no substance. You'll get our leftovers when we're done."

In Chosun there is a saying that after a family marries a daughter, there isn't even bedding left for the family. My sister was getting close to marrying age, too. What have I done, I lamented. There was only a little left of our family's savings to pay for her. A bride is supposed to bring three sets of sheets to her new family's home. Since we could only afford two, my mother had used half of the cotton from her own bedding set so I could take a third and not be shamed. My eyes scanned the room, taking in all the strange men standing along the walls of the room, Myungin's father with his crooked grin and rumpled, thinning hair, and Myungin's mother with her lipstick-stained teeth. Myungin smelled to me of betrayal. "Abuji, why did I not listen to you?" I reprimanded myself.

As was the tradition, my uncle bantered back and forth with Myungin's father that his food was not good enough and that he was going to take me away. Each time, Myungin's mother would run to get more food, including tender pork ribs, which I had never tasted before, and octopus that I had only ever seen before as pictures in books. My mouth watered, but the food was for my uncle, who would make a face each time he licked a bowl clean, then frown and exclaim again, "Not good enough! I am taking my niece away." Eventually the nongtaegi came out and the men began to get drunk.

As the evening wound to a close, my uncle and aunt asked for a few minutes alone with me. "I need to give her some advice about how to treat your son well," my uncle told Myungin's father to explain their unusual request.

When we were alone in the hallway, my uncle sighed. "I wish I didn't have to tell you this," he said, his shoulders slumping forward. "There are debts in this family to which you now belong. Those men standing to the side of the room when you came in, they were bill collectors, not relatives. Myungin's father gave them the wedding money in partial payment."

"How do you know?" I stammered.

"The collectors were fighting in another room about who got what. Myungin's father has been unable to sell many of the items he has purchased from the Chinese."

"This is why Myungin wanted to marry so fast!" my aunt cried. I looked down at my pink skirt, which was stained from the snow outside.

"What do I do?" I asked my uncle.

"You have to stay," he said. "There is nothing that can be done."

DURING THE FIRST month of our marriage, Myungin's parents were kind to me. His mother made me healthy meals of white rice, kimchi, tofu and pork soup. I had no idea where she got the food, because it was expensive and not part of their rations. It was clear from the bill collectors who came to the house every week that money was still owed. Then one day I discovered the secret. I overheard Myungin's mother boasting to a female neighbour how lucky she was to have a daughter-in-law from such a good family. "The father is an important member of the Party," Myungin's mother exclaimed. "Can you help show her how fortunate we feel by giving me some food?" she asked the woman.

The neighbour gave Myungin's mother a cucumber she had frozen from last season before.

I wanted to tell Myungin's mother that my father was not such an important member of the Party, and I likely would never be a member. I wanted them to know that I was not a good daughter. But I said nothing.

Myungin was also kind to me at first, stroking my back as I fell asleep beside him on the mat in the room along his parents' room. He gave me portions of his food to eat in the mornings before I headed to my factory job, hoping that the child inside of me was a son who would grow big. One morning, I asked Myungin if he could find me some walleye pollock, which I had eaten once when we worked in the mountains. I had a craving for it, though I knew my request would be difficult to fill. Fishermen caught the pollock near the border with Russia, but most of it was sold to the Chinese for cash, rather than rationed or sold inside Chosun. Myungin grew quiet, then he began to tell me what had happened to his father's business.

"You know that the Chinese come to Chosun to sell clothes, socks, cosmetics, towels and sweaters," he said. "Many of the things we see on the black market are originally from China. But the Chinese can never stay long before the Boweebu tells them to leave. So whatever is left, they sell to men like my father and his partner, a man he met when we left Pyongyang. The Chinese want payment for the goods up front, so my father and his partner took out a loan. Then his partner ran off with the money. My father took out a second loan to repay the first one, and then another loan to buy more items from the Chinese. But the items didn't sell."

I had never seen Myungin so distraught. He was whimpering like a baby as he spoke. For the first time since our wedding, I felt as if we belonged together.

"Because we still have debts with contacts from China," he continued, wiping away his tears, "I can't buy the pollock here. But I will get some for you from a cousin in China."

And he did. He found me enough to last for several weeks.

BUT AS THE first month of the year turned into the second, Myungin started to stay out late. When he was at home, he gave off an odour of decaying alcohol, his breath sticky and sour. I could not get close to him without vomiting from morning sickness. The foods that had nurtured me, including white rice, grew scarce. Perhaps Myungin's neighbours had nothing more to offer. The hunger pains of my childhood returned.

Myungin's mother brewed her own alcohol, selling it to neighbours who knocked on the door. She gave whatever was left over to Myungin.

I started a letter to my mother. "This house has so many secrets," I wrote. After a few sentences, I tore the paper into shreds. I didn't want to worry my parents or be disrespectful of my new family. But one day in early spring, when I had not seen Myungin in more than a week, I went to my parents' place when I finished my shift at the factory. My mother embraced me for the first time since I was a small child.

"He's been here," my father said in a stern tone. "Your husband. He came here in the middle of the night and demanded that your mother give him alcohol."

I lowered my head and covered my eyes with my hands.

"He's been sleeping in the houses of other women. Other people have seen him and told us. People we trust," my mother continued.

Tears started to stream down my face.

My father pressed on. "I told him to leave and go back to you the night he came here. Your mother gave him the alcohol because he was so angry, she was scared he was going to do something violent. You don't know this man!" he exclaimed, clenching his fists as if to punch someone.

I rubbed my belly, thinking of the child inside me. "Abuji, what do I do?"

"Go home," my mother said, setting a steaming bowl of rice in front of me. "Take these when you do." She pressed three meal tickets from my father's factory into my hand. "You need to go back and speak to him."

When I got back to my in-laws' house, Myungin was there, so drunk he could barely walk, his feet sliding out from under him, his hands slapping at the wall to prevent him from falling down. When I told him where I had been, he slapped me across the face with such force that I fell to my knees. He hit me again, this time across the back of my head. I fell forward, then quickly I rolled onto my side, worried for the baby. He came at me again, punching my face, my neck and my stomach. I held my hands in front of me for protection.

I howled like the wild wolves as he stood up and began kicking my back and stomach. His mother, in the other room, ignored my screams for help. Myungin was the head of the family now; his father had moved away to try to earn money to pay off their debts. Myungin could do anything he wanted. As he dealt out the blows, I knew I was nothing to him except a pitiful girl whose bride money was needed for his family's debts. He had never adored me. He had never cared. What hurt me most was that I had known this truth from the beginning. I just didn't want to see it.

Chapter Fourteen

AFTER THE BEATING from Myungin, I could not go to work. I didn't have the energy and I was too humiliated to see a doctor to get a medical note explaining my absence. As a result, for every day I was away, I was docked food rations. Myungin would not be happy when he went to collect our rations. But I could barely get up from my mat. My back was so badly bruised even the weight of the cotton blanket sent waves of pain through my body. But the baby survived. I had no cramps or spotting that indicated the child was in danger.

Myungin had left the house right after the attack, grabbing some bottles of alcohol on his way out. The place was quiet the next day except for Myungin's mother fussing about in the kitchen, making her nongtaegi.

But as dusk came, the house stirred. First I heard the sound of Myungin's voice, which sent shivers down my spine. I pulled my aching body up into a sitting position but was too dizzy to maintain it. I clutched the blanket in my hands and lay back down.

Then I heard my uncle's voice and the voice of my mother. I had forgotten it was Myungin's birthday. Even my father had come since it was tradition for my family to help him celebrate.

When I heard my father's brisk greeting to Myungin's mother, I decided to act.

"I'm in here," I called out. "Help me!" My cry was quiet, though, since my throat was parched. I heard cups being set down on the table and my uncle asking Myungin about his work.

I crawled toward the door. Pain ricocheted through my abdomen but I managed to turn the knob and open the door a crack. "Help me," I called out again. When my mother saw me, she screamed. I learned later that my face was covered in dark bruises as was the rest of my body.

My mother moved immediately to nurse my wounds. Once she was through, I was lying back down on my mat, the door open so I could hear the conversation.

"Let's get right to business," said my uncle. "Sunhwa is going home. How can you beat up a pregnant woman? How can you beat up your wife?"

Myungin said nothing as my mother started to wrap up my clothes. She pulled out my wedding chest and opened it. "The sheets are gone," she screeched in such a loud voice that my father and uncle came running.

"Where did everything go?" my uncle demanded of Myungin.

"We sold it," Myungin's mother replied.

There was a long silence. "What do you want us to do?" my uncle eventually asked Myungin. "Take her back, or leave her with the promise you will never do such a thing again?"

My heart sank upon hearing these words. I didn't want to stay, but I knew it would also be difficult to leave and face the shame of a failed marriage.

"What do you want, Myungin?" my uncle repeated.

By now, my mother had finished packing and was loading

things in the car that would take us back to the train station. I strained my ears to hear Myungin's decision.

"Take her back," he said finally in a gruff voice. "Just take her away. I don't want her anymore."

"I don't know what you are going to do," my mother whispered to me on the train. "Single mothers in this country have no life. No job. Nothing." She tore at the pockets of her khaki work shirt and started punching her chest. "How did it come to this?" she hissed. "Why?"

A FEW MONTHS later, at the end of planting season, I gave birth to a son. Myungin's father named him Sungmin. That very day, my mother returned to Myungin's house and begged him to apologize and then take me back. He refused at first, but in the harvest season, when Sungmin was able to hold his head up and reach out his fleshy arms when I held him close, my mother repacked my clothes in my wedding chest and took me to live with my husband again. "Neither you or the baby have a future without Myungin," she told me.

For the next three months, Myungin barely looked at his son, who had his father's eyes and my round face. And he rarely spoke to me. He was drunk most of the time. "I want another dowry," he spat one night, his spittle landing on my cheek. "I took you back. I should get compensation for my sacrifice."

It wasn't long before the beatings started. No matter how much white powder I applied to my face, nothing could conceal the bruises. Myungin hit my face with his fists. He used his belt across my back and beat the palms of my hands and the backs of my legs with a stick. His mother was almost always present, remaining quietly off to the side, refusing to look, to act, even to acknowledge my suffering.

One early morning in January, Myungin arrived home red-eyed and stinking of alcohol. He dragged me from my sleep and threw me outside in my long johns and nightshirt. My feet turned blue as I banged on the side of the house, begging to be let back in. When he finally opened the door, he threw cold water at me.

"Please stop drinking. Please consider your child," I begged. I knelt in front of him, my eyes wild, hands grasping at his trousers. But he didn't. A few nights later, he picked up Sungmin, asleep and swaddled in his blankets and dragged me by the hair to the front door. He kicked us both out. We spent the night in the neighbour's barn. Sungmin and I went back to Myungin's house, but after that my husband began to give me less and less food. There were days when all I had to eat was some turnip.

In early spring, Myungin started seeing another woman. I spotted them holding hands in the fields when I went to collect water at the well. I felt dirty, low, as if my body was part of the mud into which my torn slippers sunk.

By the time Sungmin was ten months old, I could take no more. My eyes were glassy from malnutrition, my limbs stuck in slow motion. Sungmin had a chronic cough, which I believed was from the lack of nutrients in my breast milk. One morning after Myungin had left for his job and his mother was out selling alcohol, I folded up some clothes for Sungmin, wrapped them in a pale pink bottari, and took the train back to my parents' house. I vowed this time I would never return to Myungin's home.

My mother didn't try to convince me to go back, but my father's downcast expression said it all. Myungin had brought doom to our family, haunting us like the curse of an evil ancestor. "I never believed that these evil spirits existed," my mother said one afternoon as Sungmin slept between us. "But there has been so much suffering in this family for generations."

My life since returning home was better than at Myungin's, since I was not being abused. But I could not work since I had to care for Sungmin. My child and I had no rations either. Myungin, as my husband, got our share. My mother gave us what she could but there was no money to buy us extra food.

"You need to consider adoption," she said hesitantly. "There is no other way."

I immediately started to cry.

"Your father will soon be forced to retire from the factory," she continued quietly. "He is getting old. You must return to work. You must get your life back."

"I can't," I choked out. Sungmin had just learned to walk, taking his first awkward steps a few days earlier as I helped my mother till the land for planting. His eyes sparkled in the sunlight, and his laughter warmed the dampness inside me. I felt hope deep inside me when I was with him. "Please do not make me give Sungmin away," I pleaded.

But my mother had rolled over by now, her back to me, her weak snores filling the room.

FOR THE NEXT two weeks, life went on as usual. Then one Sunday morning, my mother woke me early to ask if I could go to my uncle's house in the other part of town. "It is your cousin's birthday," she reminded me as I rolled up my mat. "Take her this." She pushed a fabric-wrapped present into my arms.

"But we have never given gifts before on our cousins' birthdays," I said, puzzled. The item was hard and heavy. I suspected it was a rice cake.

"Just do as I say," she ordered, picking up Sungmin. "I'll watch the baby."

I had to take the train to get to my uncle's house, and when I arrived, my aunt invited me to stay for white rice and kimchi. My cousin, now also a mother, rocked her newborn in her arms.

"Spend the day with me," my cousin chirped. Her lips were a soft crimson colour that reminded me of Sungmin's cheeks in the wind.

I shook my head, standing up to leave.

"You must stay," my aunt said, pulling me back down by tugging on my sleeve.

"What is going on?" I demanded. As I caught my cousin's glance darting quickly from her mother to me, a flash ran through me. Suddenly I knew why I was there, why my mother had sent me away.

I ran out the door and all the way to the train station. I paced the platform, anxious for the arrival of the carriage that would take me back to the main station in Yuseon. I thought about Myungin's anger, about my mother and her secrets. A mysterious chain of events finally became clear. My mother had spent several afternoons the week before away from home, supposedly visiting an elderly sick friend. Then, two days ago, a couple had come to our house. My mother introduced them as our new neighbours. The woman wore a wool skirt and matching jacket, her hair rolled into a smooth bun. She looked sophisticated and was dressed neatly, as if she was a high-ranking factory worker in Pyongyang, not a villager in this remote town. She stood close to me, her eyes glued to Sungmin as I fed him his porridge. "How old is he?" the woman asked.

The woman's husband put a hand on her shoulder and smiled. "Let me give you this for the child," he said to my mother, slipping some won and two bars of soap into her hand.

I had thought the couple was just being kind but now, on the train, I rolled my hand into a tight fist and hit myself hard on the leg. How could I not have figured it out? My mother was giving Sungmin away. My mother had sold him.

ONCE I GOT to Yuseon, I took the first train directly to Myungin's town. My mother could not have sold Sungmin without Myungin's permission, I knew. As the train came to a stop, I raced out onto the platform and incredibly there I saw them: Myungin, my mother, the couple who had visited our home the week before, and a woman I had never seen.

I ran toward them.

"Give him to me," I screamed, grabbing Sungmin from Myungin's arms.

Myungin stepped forward and slapped me hard across the face. As I fell to my knees, he snatched our son back.

"You can't give my child away," I sobbed.

With sympathetic eyes, the woman who was buying Sungmin searched my face.

"We will give your child a good life," her husband said sternly, pulling his wife back by the elbow and taking Sungmin from Myungin's arms. I leapt up, reaching again for my child. But Myungin was quicker and stronger than I was. He grabbed my arms and held them behind my back using his knee to force me to the ground. He held me as still as he could, though I tried to kick, as the couple got onto the train.

"No," I wailed, my voice echoing in the station.

By the time I had worked myself free from Myungin, kicking and screaming, the train was pulling away.

I grabbed the door handle and tried to hang on, running faster as the train picked up speed. But when I felt a hand grab the back of my shirt, I tumbled onto the platform. My beloved son was gone.

Part Two

Chapter Fifteen

FOR SEVERAL DAYS after Sungmin was taken, I was bedridden at my parents' house, unable to lift a spoon of rice to my mouth or even a cup of water to quench my thirst. I spent hours, as I had as a child, watching the dust dance in the beams of sunlight streaming in through the window. But unlike when I was young, my mind wasn't filled with my mother's stories of children escaping tigers. This time, my mind, body and spirit were shutting down.

Whenever I slept, I dreamt of Sungmin. I would wake gasping for air, my body soaked with sweat. Feeling as if an insect had crawled inside my head, I'd rise and go outside. I'd pace endlessly back and forth, as if the motion could banish what had taken possession of me.

I was receiving no rations, though, so after a week I had to return to work. My mother had found me a job in construction. Every morning, she forced me to drag myself out of bed. My job was to mix and then carry cement to be used in the foundation of a building. My muscles ached, but I didn't mind. The discomfort was nothing compared to the hole inside of me.

Food rations for everyone had become more scarce. Once a month, which became once in two, then three months, we were given only a bit of corn rice, some root vegetables and some cooking oil. My siblings were still finishing school, so on the days I wasn't working, I would go to the mountains with a backpack I'd made from old pants sewn together to collect herbs and grasses to supplement our meals.

"Daughter," my mother said quietly one night in early winter, as the chill from outside made its way under the doors. "These are for you." She passed me a wad of won tied with white string and two bars of soap.

"What is this for?" I asked. But I already knew. I recognized the pile of money and the soap.

"For Sungmin," my mother said, her eyes fixed on the floor. "You should at least have these things. There is a woman in town who helped me find the couple who adopted Sungmin. If you ever want to know about his health or his schooling, she will find out for you."

I counted the money, three hundred *won*, and drew in the scent of the soap. Eventually I tucked the items into my newest grey sock and placed everything in a chest I kept in the corner.

I EXISTED FOR two years in this way. I was dizzy by the end of each work day due to the lack of food, and I slept all evening. I had no social life, despite men coming to the house and asking my mother if they could meet with me. I didn't want another man. I wanted Sungmin. I clutched one of his tiny wool socks to my chest all night.

My dreams of my son had become less frequent, but I didn't want them to end. I would often lie half-awake on my mat, remembering everything I could about him, every detail of our brief life together. Sometimes, when I awoke, I would think I felt Sungmin on top of me, lying on my chest. I would sob uncontrollably when I realized he was not there. In my mind's eye,

I saw him getting bigger, muscles forming on his little arms, his eyes lighting up when he was given some porridge or his hair was stroked.

One day, I gathered my courage and asked my mother for the address of the woman who had organized the adoption.

Over those two years, my mother had slowly broken down. Hunger was the cause, I believed. Her back was hunched, her eyes sunken with fatigue. Every member of our family, from youngest to oldest, had ribs that poked out, showing through our cotton shirts in summer. Our cheekbones stood out like sticks. We survived mainly on dandelion stems and grass sautéed in soy sauce. And we weren't alone. Hunger was sweeping the neighbourhood.

I WALKED ACROSS town to the address my mother had given me, arriving with rain dripping down my face. I knocked on the woman's door as I rehearsed what I wanted to say: "I'm Sunhwa. Two years ago, you gave my child away. I would like to know how he is doing? Where he went and in what kind of home he is being raised?"

The woman opened the door and squinted at me. I stood silent, too afraid to speak, but her face softened after a minute. "I remember you," she said pulling me inside.

The woman had me sit while she heated some water. When she was done, we sipped tea made with herbs from the mountains as I asked about Sungmin. She knew little about the couple, other than that they had no children at the time they adopted Sungmin. "When your child is a bit older, they want to adopt a second child, a girl," she said. "Sungmin will have a sister?" I exclaimed.

"Yes, one day," replied the woman. "Though he will not be Sungmin anymore. I'm sure they gave your son a new name.

STARS BETWEEN THE SUN AND MOON

They were a good family. Be happy for your son. No doubt he is well cared for."

"Where . . . where . . . " I stammered, not wanting to give my true intentions away.

"They live somewhere in Wonsan," she said. "The father works in the navy."

The naval base in Wonsan, I knew, patrolled the waters off the eastern coast, in case the south tried to invade Chosun.

As I walked away from the woman's home, I touched the money tied with the string and the soap I carried in my pocket. I had wrapped them in a plastic bag to protect them from the rain. With my socks soaking wet from the holes in my boots, I headed straight home to talk to my brother Hyungchul.

"I have the information we need," I told him when he arrived home from school. Over the past few days, while my mother slept, we had come up with a plan. My brother and I were going to find Sungmin and buy him back. We didn't tell anyone, because we knew they would protest against our plan. I knew when Sungmin was in my arms again, no one could refuse him.

My sister was preparing to get married. But she and her future husband were happy. He was a kind man, and despite having to forgo many wedding traditions because of my family's poverty, he accepted and loved my sister. That afternoon, Hyungchul and I told my mother, my sister and her fiancé that we would be leaving for a few days.

"Where are you going?" my sister asked.

My brother jumped in. "To a place in the mountains to find food."

On our way out after packing a few things, we found my mother in the garden. As I stood before her to say goodbye, a flood of guilt washed over me. I couldn't lie anymore: I told her that we were going to find Sungmin. "I am going to buy him

132

back," I said. I spoke in the most confident tone I could muster, though I knew I was defying my parents by my actions.

I thought my mother would be angry at the news, so I turned away quickly. But her response was not what I expected. "I will support you," she said in a quiet voice. I turned back and looked into her tired face. I wanted to thank her, but I also couldn't forget what she had done. I shook my head in confusion.

WHEN MY BROTHER and I arrived in Wonsan, the capital city of Gangwon province, the sun was setting, casting long shadows across the cement apartment buildings. We spent the night on the floor of the train station.

The next morning, we went straight to the naval headquarters. But the iron gate across the front was closed, and the guards would not let me in. I walked around the large compound trying to find another way in. There was none. I went back to the front gate three times that day, my face flushed with anxiety and the anticipation of finding the man who called my child his son. I pleaded with the guards to let me enter. But I didn't know the man's name. His place of work was the only information I had.

Hyungchul and I got to the naval base as early as we could the next morning. We stood outside, searching the faces of the men arriving there to work. When that proved fruitless, we began going from one neighbourhood to another, searching desperately for the couple. I asked every person we saw if they knew a man who worked at the naval base and was father to an adopted four-year-old boy. After a while, our feet were covered in blisters, our clothes stained with perspiration and dust.

"We'll ask the people in other neighbourhoods on our next visit to Wonsan," Hyungchul consoled me at the end of the fourth day. I was distraught as I pulled my bottari in close to my body, testing with my fingers to make sure that the soap and money were still on top. Hyungchul lit a cigarette as we walked slowly back to the train station. Our search had been unsuccessful but we could not stay away from work any longer.

OUR FATHER SCOLDED us harshly when we got back to our family home. "The reason why so much bad luck has come to you, Sunhwa, is because you don't pay your respects to the dead," he snapped. "When we go to the tombs of your ancestors in the mountain, all you do is eat the food we bring to honour them."

Every spring, on Kim Il-sung's birthday and in the fall, during *Chuseok*, the harvest festival and Ancestor Day, my family headed along with many others to the mountain, where our ancestors were buried under big mounds of earth. We would stand in a line facing their tomb, bowing and paying our respects in a ceremony. But my father was right. I was always more interested in the feast that the women who had made the journey prepared together.

"The ghosts of your ancestors are upset," my father continued in a piercing voice, "because you do not visit them."

I was despondent. "Can I do anything to change my fate?" I asked, sliding onto my knees and clutching my hands in front of me.

My father waved me away as he turned toward his room. Once he had shut his door, my mother spoke up. "I know a fortune teller. I will give you the money to see her."

"No, no," I protested, thinking of the money my mother earned selling the tofu she made at home. It was all she and my father had to buy the extra food they needed.

"It's fine," she assured me, slipping ten won into my pocket from her own. "Rations will be coming soon. You need to see this woman. She will tell you what ghosts are haunting you."

I TOLD ONLY one other person about my impending visit to the fortune teller: my friend Gilok, a neighbour who lived not far from our house. She was younger than I was, and struggling too. Her first child, a son, had died within two days of his birth. Gilok was pregnant with her second child now, but fearful she would lose it as well.

"Why should I go with you?" she asked, playing with a piece of a grass. We were sitting outside by the river, away from anyone who might overhear.

"Umma says the fortune teller will tell me which ghosts are with me," I explained. "Maybe she can do that for you too, so your second baby will be born healthy."

All my mother knew about this fortune teller was that she was old and that she lived in a village located a half day's walk from our own. In case we couldn't find the old woman immediately, Gilok and I planned to spend the night in the train station. We each packed food in a bottari, and, not wanting to leave it behind, I tucked in the money and the soap from Sungmin's adoption. After taking two trains, we walked along mud paths through the hills to the village. By the time we arrived, our faces were streaked with dirt.

Suddenly I felt someone breathing close behind me as we walked along the main road. I turned to face a large woman whose wrinkled face and sunken eyes put her age at well over ninety.

"You are looking for me," she said in a deep voice that reminded me of frogs croaking.

"I . . . I . . . " My lips and throat were dry from nervousness. "How did you know?"

"The spirit told me poor people were coming to see me," she replied. "The spirit also told me I needed to come and greet you."

The woman wobbled on legs that bowed like my cousin Heeok's had as a child. She led us through a town of white cement houses with brown tile roofs and patched windows. When we reached her home, she had us sit in a darkened room. The only furniture was a set of drawers, a mat and a small round wooden table.

The woman used a crooked stick to help lower her body into a seated position. Once she was settled, she stared for a long time at Gilok.

"Before you were married, your husband dated another woman," she eventually said. "She is the reason you are having problems with your babies."

Gilok's sadness poured out, tears streaming down her face. "How do you know this?" she cried.

"The spirits. Always the spirits," the fortune teller replied. "But your husband married you instead. The other woman died from grief, and her ghost has cursed any child that comes from you, including the one inside you now." She pointed to Gilok's stomach. "By the time your next son recognizes your face, he will die, too."

"No," Gilok yelled, her fists pounding the small table in front of us.

The fortune teller turned next to me.

"You," she said, "the child you seek is happy. He calls another woman mother and another man father. They love him. He loves them. He is precious to those parents. Don't look for him anymore." She spoke forcefully, shaking her head. "When he is military age, he might come to look for you."

"How can my friend and I change our futures?" I pleaded.

I reached for the woman's hand, but she quickly drew back.

"You will take your shoes off three times," she continued, ignoring my question, "and you will get married three times."

"Please tell us how we can avoid our fates," Gilok choked out.

"I can do a spell for you, a *boojeok*," the woman said, looking at Gilok. "But it will cost you each three hundred won."

"I will do it. I will do it," Gilok cried, pulling a sock out of her bottari. Inside was some won, which she threw across the table. "Do whatever you have to do."

"And you?" the fortune teller asked me.

I felt as if the breath had been knocked out of my body. The money I carried was Sungmin's adoption money. If I gave it to the fortune teller, I would have no chance of buying Sungmin back. "I need to get the won from home," I replied, my mind imagining Sungmin in the arms of another mother. "May I have some time to think about this?"

"Yes," said the fortune teller. "You always know where to find me."

I KNEW I was never going back to the fortune teller, even after Gilok gave birth to a son who lived. Two years passed, and I tried as best I could to hold on to my dreams of finding Sungmin. I spent much of my time foraging in the mountains for shrubs and herbs that my family could share. One day in a mountain village, I bumped into the woman who had sold Sungmin. I begged her for more information. She got angry with me and told me to never return. Her neighbour overheard the conversation and as I walked back to my family's house, she caught up with me.

"Don't be sad," she whispered. "Your child is safe and doing well. He is very handsome."

Stunned, I stared at the woman not sure what to say next. "How do you know?" I finally asked.

"Because that woman who sold your child is the adoptive mother's younger sister. Your son came to visit once."

My knees felt like collapsing. My throat became dry. I wiped my perspiring brow.

"Will you come and get me next time they come back?" I finally managed to get out.

"I'll try," she said, as I wrote, with shaking hands, directions to where I lived on a tattered piece of paper. "But they have only come once. Look at you, though," she then said before I could ask any more questions about my son. "The people who are raising him are good, loyal, hard working and have food. He's better off where he is, if just for a little while."

I looked down at my dirty, torn clothes. I stretched my hands, with their broken fingernails and calluses, out in front of me.

The fortune teller was right. I had to leave Sungmin where he was. I would confuse him now by telling him who he really was. He is better off in the home of people who cared for him, I thought, than in my frail arms. Filled with the deepest sorrow, I turned away.

Chapter Sixteen

FROM THEN ON, I endured my construction job without complaint, despite the calluses on my hands, the blisters on my feet, the clothes that stank of sweat, and the dried cement embedded in my matted hair. At least when I was busy, I could escape the pain that haunted my nights, spent longing for Sungmin. Even my physical hunger, growing worse with each day, was a reprieve from the hunger in my soul.

The construction team and I took our breaks at a small house down the road. The men talked and smoked as I sat hunched in the corner, listening to their conversations. Most of their talk revolved around the food they were lacking and the reasons why we were all suffering so much.

"People are quitting their jobs everywhere," said a thin man whose knobby elbows poked through his coat.

"Why bother working?" exclaimed another. "There are no rations on the shelves and we have no energy for physical labour."

"It's the Americans, the awful Americans. They're in cahoots with South Koreans to destroy us," snapped a third comrade, a man with veins on his hands sticking out like rivers. "The Americans are starving us to death."

One afternoon as I was taking a few sips of the cold water the homeowners had left in a bucket for us, I spied a bowl of white rice in an open cupboard. I had never thought of stealing from the people who lived here before, but my stomach ached from starvation and from the weeds we were now eating every day as our main source of food. After my co-workers had left the house, butting out their cigarettes in a metal can full of sand, I scooped a handful of the rice into the palm of my hand. In the outhouse, which had not been cleaned for a long time, I shoved the uncooked rice into my mouth and swallowed it without chewing.

EVERY WEEK, MY co-workers and I attended a seminar at which the Party secretary of our company would inform us about the famine. "It is because of the Americans," he would always explain, his voice harsh, his legs set stiffly side by side. The Party secretary's uniform was clean, unlike our work or home clothes, which were full of holes and dirty. Most people had only a few changes of shirts and pants now, having sold the rest for rice and vegetables. "You all need to exhibit heightened revolutionary awareness," the secretary would belt out. "Do not heed false rumours. There are spies from the outside planting these."

"What kind of rumours?" I whispered once to a colleague.

"Don't you know?" she replied with a snarl. "That there are no more food rations, that people in Pyongyang are being fed well while we in the countryside suffer."

I looked at the Party secretary's round face and rosy cheeks. He was healthy. But when I scanned the workers, I could see that the skin on our faces caved into the crevices between our bones. We were covered in small rashes and wounds. A comrade on the construction site was having difficulty seeing out of one eye. None of us wanted him to lose his job, so we would guide him through his duties, pointing him to areas where he needed to smooth out the wet concrete.

"The United States is interfering with our trade activities," the Party secretary intoned. "They are the ones to blame."

I no longer had much idea what month, day or even year it was. It was easier to forget, because remembering meant thinking about how old Sungmin was now. He would be speaking in full sentences, starting school, lifting a pen and writing his name. "His name," I thought so many times. "I wonder what it is now?"

For that reason, I was not sure exactly what month it was when our great leader Kim Il-sung died. The day before we learned of his death, my mother had travelled out to the farm area and bought a box of forty eggs with money she had earned from selling tofu. It was a windfall to find just one egg, let alone so many. She soaked the eggs in cold water overnight so that they would peel easily.

Early the next morning, I helped her boil the eggs. It was raining by the time we were done.

My mother, who walked with a limp by now, was not well enough to spend a day hawking eggs at the train station by herself. People were just not showing up to work, including me, so I could go with my mother and help. We tried to keep dry by wrapping plastic around ourselves, but the only plastic we had at home was full of holes. By the time we arrived at the train station, we could wring water from the hems of our shirts.

We planned to catch the workers on their way to the factories. But many people were at the train station for the same reason we were: to sell what food they had in exchange for food they were missing in their diets. When the rain stopped at noon, I sent my mother home, promising her I would sell the remaining eggs to the evening shift workers.

Once she had gone, I sat down for the first time that day and closed my eyes to take a nap. Soon I felt a sharp kick in the thigh. I opened my eyes to see a security guard pointing a stick at me. "You need to move," he ordered.

"But I must sell my eggs," I protested, showing him the bag they were in. "Would you like one?"

The guard hit me sharply on the back with his stick. "I will kill you if you remain," he hissed. As I stood to go, he spun around and pushed me toward the exit.

Out on the street, there were uniformed men everywhere. Some were walking in military stride. Others patrolled the streets. Never before had I seen so many members of the Party out and about. "Maybe war has come," I thought. "I must get home to my mother." But then my thoughts turned to an even more pressing concern. I had not sold all the eggs, and my family was dependent on that. I had to find a way back into the station to sell the rest.

Then as I turned the corner, I heard the shocking announcement: the voice of a man, booming out from a radio, said that Kim Il-sung had died.

I crept toward the window of the home where the radio was playing, stood on a rock and peered inside. I nearly fell off the rock when I saw that it wasn't a radio at all, but a colour television. Some of my friends' families had black and white television sets. I'd even watched *Robinson Crusoe* once at Pumpkin's house. But I had never seen a set that gave off pictures in colour, though my father had told me about them. The families who owned them probably had relatives living in China before liberation, he had explained. The only other way a rural person could own such a thing was if their family had had gold from before the revolution. After liberation, my father explained, they would have been asked by the Party to exchange their gold for won and they could have used that to purchase a colour television from one of the markets.

I stepped down off the rock, my eyes filling with tears. I felt as if my own father had died. I passed others on the street who were crying like I was. By the time I made it to my family's home, all my eggs had been sold to passersby. But I was so weak with grief, I collapsed on the floor.

That next morning, filled with sadness, I donned my wedding outfit. My mother and I used our money from the eggs to buy chrysanthemums from a flower shop. The young woman who sold us the flowers was also dressed in a traditional skirt and top. My entire family and I then went together by train to my father's factory. Although all the carriages were full, not a single person spoke. The only sound was muffled crying.

The workers and their families gathered in the factory's auditorium. One by one, people moved toward the centre of the room, where a large photograph of Kim Il-sung had been hung, to lay their flowers. Many flung themselves to the ground and wailed so loudly my ears rang from the noise. When it was my family's turn, my own cries joined with the others. I cried for Kim Il-sung, I cried for the flower girl, I cried for our freedom, I cried for our hunger, I cried for Sungmin.

For the next ten days, no one was allowed to speak in a loud voice, even inside their homes. No one went to work. The Party informed us via radio and television that we were not allowed to congregate with more than one other person at a time, except in our homes, and even then it had to be family. "Our dear leader has given us great provisions," my father said softly one night. "We owe much to him."

Every morning, I bathed in cold water, then slipped into my wedding outfit and put white powder on my cheeks. Then my family and I would again go to my father's factory. Like everyone else there, we remained silent except when we cried in front of Kim Il-sung's portrait.

After ten days of mourning, we waited for Kim Jong-il, Kim Il-sung's son to instruct the nation what to do next.

We had always known Kim Jong-il would someday take over from his father. Most of our classes at school were conducted using the leather books containing the words and teachings of our dear leader. But some of the books had also been written by his son.

One of Kim Jong-il's teachings was a question posed in a song he had penned for his father. "Time stays the same for everyone," he had written, "but the clock on my father's desk, why does it move so hurriedly?"

In class, I had flung my hand in the air to say I felt the meaning of the line was that our eternal father needed to slow down and rest. "He's working too hard to protect and serve us," I said. "The song shows the son's great love for his father. He wants his father to look after his health."

From the photographs hung in classrooms and factories, I knew that Kim Jong-il had the same square jaw, tiny eyes and wide forehead as his father. They wore the same kind of black-rimmed eyeglasses, and both of them had lots of fat on their bodies. Of course, they would always get food first. They had to look after us, and so needed the most energy of all. I could not imagine them doing their important work feeling the way I did every day, lugging my body out of bed, my head fuzzy from lack of food, my thoughts spiralling every which way, tears erupting from deep inside whenever I saw a boy the same age as Sungmin.

FAMILY, NEIGHBOURS AND colleagues: we all waited for Kim Jong-il to address us. But word from Pyongyang did not come.

Months passed, but the newspapers were silent. People's hunger grew worse. Our monthly rations shrunk until they were enough to last only a week. There were days my family survived solely on water. And flooding from the rains brought disease. People broke out in rashes that became infested with maggots. Many had constant colds, flus and chronic coughs. People began to leave our neighbourhood, dragging their tired bodies out to the rural areas, hoping to find food there. Children struggled to keep up with their parents, their faces drawn, their skin blackened and flaking off. Everyone looked decades older than they actually were. We were dying. All of us.

My mother recounted a terrible story from the neighbourhood one night as we sat together in flickering candlelight. The electricity was long gone. A few blocks over, she said, a man had married a young woman who was fat and short. Her new mother-in-law felt the woman was eating too much, so she kicked her out of the house. My mother wiped tears from her eyes as she continued. "The young woman ate whatever she could find in the river: tadpoles, worms. She couldn't go home. I gave her some tofu, but I had only a little to spare. She became so bloated she lost all her strength and could only crawl. She found her way to an abandoned house, and her husband discovered her a few days later, after she had died. People say the young woman's body was rolled up in a sheet and taken to the mountain, where it was left to rot. But the mother-in-law prepared a table for her of whatever food the family could find, including some of my tofu. They didn't want to be cursed by her spirit."

All around us, people's personalities had changed. Vendors on the street had their bread and eggs stolen. People sold their clothes and furniture in the rural areas in exchange for vegetables. With no more rations, everything had turned mad.

I quit my job, telling my supervisor that I was getting married and moving away. I needed to help my mother, to make sure people didn't rob her. I spent my days walking back and forth to the train station, ever watchful of limber young boys who would snatch our tofu and shove it in their mouths before I could even scold them.

Finally, in hushed conversations, people started to question whether our hunger really was caused by the Americans. People wanted to know why Kim Jong-il would not speak. Some defended the regime, saying Kim Jong-il was respecting the three-year mourning period, *sahm-nyun-sahng.*

And, indeed, he may have been. Three years after Kim Il-sung's death—three years of decay, in which even our summer sunlight did little to lighten the black and grey hues of life in Chosun—Supreme Leader Kim Jong-il issued a statement. He reminded us of the Arduous March, the slogan from our war of liberation with the Japanese. The slogan was coined after Kim Il-sung, leading his soldiers, marched through the Chinese border provinces near Chosun, fighting against ten thousand enemy soldiers for over one hundred days during a battle against the Japanese. All the while, his soldiers were dying from lack of food, the plague and low spirits. Kim Il-sung shared whatever food he had with his soldiers and encouraged everyone to press on. He said that victory was near, and it was.

In Kim Jong-il's first official instruction, communicated via the Party, he said that we, all of Chosun, were on an Arduous March much like his father and his soldiers had been. Because of the rains and the flooding, Chosun was in the midst of a nation-wide famine. We must fight through this, he commanded us. We must fight through this and win.

Chapter Seventeen

FROM THE DAY our great father's son, whom we called the General, emboldened us to take up the mantle of the Arduous March, we mustered our nerve, put aside our worries and dug in deep. We also started receiving information about the rest of the world over the radio and in our newspapers, learning that the USSR had become capitalist, driven by greedy oligarchs. We, the people of Chosun, the government told us, were susceptible to the same fate.

"There are black clouds on the horizon. Winds of temptation gush over us," a radio broadcaster announced. "The capitalists want Chosun to fall."

These words became part of a song that was played over and over on the radio and at marches held in Pyongyang in support of the Arduous March. Veterans of the Korean War came out into the streets wearing their uniforms. I watched on a neighbour's black and white television set as they saluted while marching past the General. Kim Jong-il praised the soldiers' absolute loyalty and said the veterans would lead the fight against the capitalists.

"If the Americans come, we will be ready," people shouted in the streets.

A movie called *Nation and Fate* was released in the cinemas. The story was about North Koreans who lived abroad, travelling from one major city to another, only to realize that Chosun was the best place on earth for them. South Korean president Park Chung-hee was shown in the movie to illustrate the evils of capitalism. "Why would anyone want to hurt our dear leader? This leader of the puppet army in the south must be a horrible person," I overheard people in the train station saying to each other.

Kim Jong-il continually told the people, via the Party, that things would get better. I believed him. But until they did, we had to survive.

ONE DAY, DURING a planting season in which not much was being planted, I managed to sell all of my mother's tofu by noon. I decided to spend the afternoon visiting a friend from the neighbourhood who had wed and moved to a nearby village.

Rina was younger than I was and taller than most men, with a long neck and perfect white teeth. She spoke gently, like I imagined a deer would talk if it could.

She took me into the back room of her small dark house, which was cool despite the warm temperature outside, and began whispering, leaning in so close I could smell her breath. "I hear if we take seafood to China, we can exchange it for other food. I've heard that if we go to Chongjin we can buy the seafood there. Then we take a train ride to Samjang. We cross the Tumen River into Adong in China, knock on doors and sell the seafood in exchange for corn and white rice. We can get across the river into China and back without being caught. Lots of people are doing it now."

I gasped, placing my hand over my mouth. I pulled Rina in so close our cheeks touched. "What happens if you get caught?"

"No one has been caught," she whispered. "You should come with me," she urged with a nod. "You can feed your whole family."

The committee leader who oversaw the behaviour of my family and our neighbours in thirty other houses had recently told me that I had to either get married or find a bona fide job. However, my mother was ailing, and there would be very few rations available even if I went to work. Our only chance was if I remained with my mother and helped her to sell what she cooked. She would die trying to do that without me.

There was no way I was going to be with a man again, that much I had vowed. My life was serving my mother and surviving this famine that was taking the lives of more and more people, including my mother's best friend, a timid woman who had left behind eight children. My life was living for the day Sungmin came to look for me, like the fortune teller had said. If I had to go back to a job, I would also be unable to hunt for the roots and herbs I found deep in the forest. Life was terrible in Chosun. Whenever I went to the rural areas, I would see children digging through animal waste for corn kernels or other solid pieces of food, which they would wash in the river and then eat.

I was terrified, but I knew I had to do what Rina proposed.

WHEN THE DAY came to buy the fish and then head to Adong, Rina was sick. Her breathing was laboured. Her chest, I could hear, was full of liquid. I had brought all the money I had saved from selling my mother's tofu. I felt I couldn't turn back, so legs shaking with fear, I walked to Chongjin alone along the hilltop paths to buy some mackerel. There, I waited for the train to take me to the border town of Samjang.

I waited and waited on the platform under the high spring sun, my clothes stuck to my back with perspiration.

I sat down and placed the bag full of frozen mackerel in my shadow in an attempt to keep it cool. "Fuel shortage," one of the military guards patrolling the platform said to me. "No coal. The train may not come for days." He jangled some metal objects in the pocket of his crisp new khaki pants.

My bag was wet by now, the ice melting off the mackerel. I didn't have days to wait. I had hours, or else the fish would go bad and all our money would be gone. My entire family would starve. There was nothing I could do. I went back to the market and sold the fish for half the price I had paid for it. I used the money to buy some sugar, which I knew I could sell for double the price back in my neighbourhood to make up what I had lost.

Night fell as I walked past the train station. Just then a train pulled up. I was so tired my body sank into the seat, and I dozed off.

"I know your mother and sister," I heard someone say. I opened my eyes to see the wrinkled face of an older lady. I had never seen this woman before, with the bald spots on her head and her scalp bleeding in places. But then again, everyone looked so different from how they had appeared before the Arduous March began.

The woman smiled, revealing missing teeth, and started naming off my siblings. But she was no friend. I got up to go to the washroom as the train jolted its way into the first station. When I got back, I discovered that the woman had departed, taking with her my backpack and my sugar.

I couldn't go home with nothing to give my family. I had to find some food with the tiny bit of money I had left in my pocket. I got off the train and headed back to Chongjin on foot, my head throbbing, my body shaking from nerves and fatigue. I wanted to pull my own hair out for letting everyone down.

I slept in an alleyway that night. The next morning, I bought some rice. I sold the rice for corn, then bought an egg that I sold for a pepper and so on. The market was full of people with dirty fingernails and dirt stains on their faces and who smelled of sweat and urine. Desperate, I had to keep going for as long as it took me. My only food was a bowl of noodles at the end of each day. All I had to drink was the broth in which the noodles were cooked. But I was driven by my goal to barter and trade until I made up for my family what I had lost.

One afternoon, after about a week of this, I felt a hand on my shoulder as I was trading some turnip. I turned and looked into the worried eyes of my mother.

"I thought you had died," she said, a tear streaking her dirty cheek. "Come home."

"I lost everything," I confessed. I wanted to collapse but I held myself steady.

"No, you didn't. The old woman you met on the train brought your sugar to us. She said you got up from your seat and never came back."

"That's not true," I said wildly. But part of me was uncertain of my words. I had heard that lack of food sometimes played tricks with the mind. Perhaps I had not gone back to the right train compartment?

"Come home," my mother whispered.

THE NEXT MORNING, I packed the sugar in my backpack and headed to the market.

"What are you selling?" a woman about my mother's age asked as I turned the corner. I shook my head, indicating I had nothing. The woman wasn't carrying anything, and I suspected she had nothing to trade. I tried to push past her to get to the market, but she blocked my way. Beside her stood a younger woman holding a baby.

"What are you selling?" she asked again.

My hands started to shake. I was fearful they wanted to rob me. "Sugar," I said, placing my backpack on the ground and undoing the fraying string I had used to tie the top.

"I'll buy the whole bag," the woman said. My eyes grew wide.

"I know people in Adong," she continued. "I'll sell it there and give you the money when I get back—double what you would make at the market."

"No," I replied, grabbing the sugar and stuffing it back in the bag. The woman stepped closer to me, her hand on the bag. "Please don't take my sugar," I pleaded. "It's all my family has."

The woman stared at me, her eyes cold. The younger woman with the baby stepped toward me, too. There was no one else around. We were on a deserted part of the road.

"Fine," I said in a shaky voice. "But only if I go with you."

I WAS SO nervous I urinated in the river as we crossed over to China. My steps were as heavy as if I was walking in cement. But in the dark of the night through which we travelled, I knew I would lose the women if I didn't keep up with them. So I lifted my feet, time after time from the muddy bottom of the Tumen River.

When we reached the shore on the other side, I followed the two women out. Under a tree, we slipped off our pants and wrung the water out, then did the same with our shirts. After we had dressed again in damp clothes, we knocked on the doors of some houses the women said belonged to ethnic Koreans, people originally from Chosun who had lived in China since before the revolution. I was no longer afraid. I felt greedy as I watched the women exchange my sugar for white rice. We returned when the night was the blackest, wading back across the river to Chosun.

A few days later, Myungsook, a teenager who travelled from the rural area where she lived to sell eggs at the train station, told me that you get as much as a kilo of white rice in trade for one puppy in China. That was nearly triple what I had got for my sugar. "And one kilo of white rice, you can sell for 1,000 won," Myungsook said, smiling like Pumpkin would when sharing stories of boys and forbidden romance.

That afternoon, we each purchased a puppy in a nearby town. Mine was black with a white foot. Myungsook's dog was mud brown. This time we crossed the river halfway between two towns as the sun was setting. I waded more confidently. The rocks on the bottom of the river were slippery, though, and I stumbled a few times. I was afraid I would lose the puppy, which I had concealed in my backpack with its head poking out so it could breathe.

When we reached the other side, we wrung our clothes out. Then we followed forest paths along the river to a different town than the one I had visited before. Whenever we saw lights coming our way on the town streets, Myungsook whispered for me to duck behind a garbage bin or down an alleyway. "Patrol cars," she told me. "If they get you, they will send you back across the bridge to Chosun and then to prison."

Just as we had finished knocking at the tenth house, a voice announced over a PA system that it was dinnertime. The streets cleared instantly, and everything turned quiet.

Myungsook rapped her knuckles on the door a second time. We were turning to leave when we heard footsteps. A fat man opened the wooden door and beamed from ear to ear when he saw the dogs' heads peeking out from our bags. He waved for us to follow him into the kitchen, where his wife and two young daughters were eating noodles.

I licked my lips as I handed my puppy to the man. But when he snapped his fingers, his wife took her bowl, which I saw included rice and peppers, and placed it on the floor for the dog to eat.

I couldn't hide my shock. All of Chosun was starving, yet in China ethnic Koreans fed dogs with food right from their tables. Myungsook and I filled our backpacks with soybean paste, peppers and white rice. We left the house without eating, since no food was offered.

Chapter Eighteen

"I'M GOING TO leave," I said to my sister one night during the harvest season.

We were lying on the ground under a bridge in Chongjin, covered in plastic tarps to protect us from the cold. Sunyoung had come with me to trade tofu for some pollock, if she could find any. Her daughter, who was almost five, was in size no larger than a toddler, her legs bowed with the rickets that afflicted so many children in the country now. I had bought my niece a little fabric doll with one eye missing in China. I was travelling there at least once a week now to trade food.

"For good?" Sunyoung asked.

"No, just for a few months. I am going to find Father's distant relatives, who have been living in China since before the revolution, and collect lots of food and money from them. You should see how people eat, how they live, on the other side!" I said enthusiastically. "The children are fat. The women have hips. The men have stomachs, and the dogs eat food from the table."

"But we don't know where these relatives are. We've only ever heard rumours about them," she said. When I didn't reply, she continued: "When are you going to go?"

"Soon," I said.

After that we lay in silence, listening to the heavy snores of the men and women who had crowded under the bridge like us, finding refuge at night in places that in the past would have been unthinkable. People slept there and sought food by day, however they could, even if that meant stealing.

To travel out of town for more than a few train stops, you needed to get a permit from the government office at work. It had always been difficult for us to acquire the proper papers to visit our grandparents in Hoeryong or family friends who lived elsewhere because each workplace was only allowed to issue a certain number of permits. But we eventually received them. Now, so many more people were applying for permits to travel to trade things secretly and find food. Unless one bribed the issuing official or had connections, it was becoming almost impossible to get a permit to travel at all.

By now, I was trading our old shoes, pants and sweaters in the rural areas for turnip and cabbage. There was little food left in my own town, so we had no choice but to sneak onto the trains. Train stations that had once had two guards inspecting permits now had four. But the guards usually started by checking the permits of passengers at the back of the train.

There were dozens of us illegal passengers. The men and women who still worked for the government tried to maintain their appearance, smoothing down their brittle hair with oils and washing and ironing their uniforms. Some others, who had connections or money and could regularly obtain travel permits even though they were travelling to sell things illegally like me, were also on the train, neat and confident. But those of us who were travelling illegally stood out. Our dirty feet and fingernails, our tangled hair and our large backpacks sewn from old clothes were easy to spot.

We would huddle together, one train away from the guards. As the guards moved forward to the next carriage, so did we. When we reached the final carriage, we would run back along the platform as fast as we could and scatter ourselves throughout the other carriages. The guards would always catch one or two of us—never me, so far. The culprit would be jailed and made to pay fifty won to be released.

BEFORE I LEFT to seek my father's relatives, I wanted to make sure my parents had enough food to last them for a few months, both to eat and to trade. I boarded a train heading to Chongjin, my arms full of the white rice I had picked up on my last trip to China. I planned to trade it for fish and vegetables.

On the last part of the journey, which I made on foot, I bumped into Myungin on the street. We stared at each other, speechless. He seemed to have aged twenty years. He was so thin I could see his ribcage through his thick sweater. He seemed inches shorter and his eyes popped out of his angular face. He smiled, revealing rotting teeth. He, too, was on his way to market, trying to sell produce.

"I'm married again," he told me.

I said nothing as I scanned his face for signs of remorse or guilt.

"We never registered our marriage, you know, you and I."

"I remember," I replied, uncertain why he was disclosing all of this.

"I couldn't have divorced you so easily if our marriage had been registered," he then said as if it was his atonement. "You wouldn't have had your life back."

I was surprised both at his admission and at the lack of care I felt for him. I had no love left but no hate for him, either. I was neither happy nor sad about his declaration. I discovered something in that moment: I had never loved him. By contrast, my feelings for Sungmin, the bond of eternity, was a love that would never be broken, an invisible rope connecting us always.

I thought of asking Myungin if he knew anything about our son but decided against it. I didn't want to know the answer. If he had been in contact with Sungmin's new family, I would feel rage. Sungmin belonged to me, not him. Myungin had never cared about him. But if he had not been in contact, then I would fear for Sungmin's safety. I liked this new experience of not having emotions. I avoided asking questions that might bring pain. I had learned to live as a ghost.

"My father heard you had been arrested and were in prison again," I said, changing the subject.

"Yes," he admitted. "I stole a pig from a farm with four friends. I traded it for 3,000 won."

I gasped. There was very little livestock left in Chosun.

"One of the men I was caught with told the police that I was the leader. I was tortured and beaten." His words trailed off.

"I would forgive you your crime." I surprised myself with the thought. I saw Myungin's vulnerability as he shifted from foot to foot, wringing his scarred hands. He no longer seemed the monster I had married but a small, frightened boy, suffering the way we all were.

"That man had several children at home to feed," Myungin went on, "whereas I only have a small daughter. My wife sells tofu. I did my time in prison to save my friend."

Myungin had wronged me. I waited for the words "I am sorry" to come from his mouth. However, it was not to be.

"I must go," he said. He limped off down the dirt road. I watched until I could no longer see his back, his body sinking down the hill.

I NEEDED TO find out, without telling my mother my true intentions, the names of my father's relatives rumoured to live in China. I broached the subject with her one afternoon as she mended a hole in one of my father's few remaining cotton shirts. I had helped her thread the needle, since her eyes were too weak to see the needle's eye.

"Do you ever wish you had met your grandfather and uncle?" I began. "The ones who went to China? What are their names?"

My mother gave me their names. "But they didn't go to China. They went to South Korea," she said, falling right into my plan. "They went where they were not supposed to go."

Getting into South Korea was impossible now; that much I knew. Heading south meant travelling through militarized land, skirting landmines and guards who would stand me in front of a firing squad if I were caught. "But your father has relatives in China," my mother said, just like I had hoped. "They left long, long before the revolution. They live in a place called Hadong Orchard."

"What are their names?" I asked in a timid voice.

"I don't know," she said.

I struggled to hide my disappointment.

A few days later, I announced to my mother that I was going to travel to the countryside for a while, trading food. I told only my sister where I was really going, reassuring her that I would be fine. I had travelled across the river to China many times by now.

"You're never going to find these relatives," my sister said. "China is a big place. You don't know their names."

I couldn't allow her words to discourage me. "I have to try."

WHEN I MADE it across the river, soaking wet, I pulled myself up on the banks of a small town, ducking into an alley just as

a Chinese security guard rounded the corner. It was dinnertime, usually the best time to cross into China, since most of
the guards took a break to eat. But the Chinese were cracking
down on illegals like me entering the country now, and there
was more security than ever.

I stood with my back flush against the clay wall of a house
and held my breath as the guard walked past. I could see his
rifle when he was in front of me, and I nearly let out a scream,
because my footprints and droplets of water on the sandy road
were still visible. But he did not look to the side, just straight
ahead. He did not see me.

When he was gone, I snuck down the alley and climbed over
a few fences. Night had fallen, and the harvest moon was low,
casting a dull orange light over the road. I rapped my knuckles
on the door of the only house I knew: the man to whom I had
sold the puppy. After that, he had repeatedly bought the fish
and other goods from Chosun I brought to China.

"Please," I begged when he opened the door, his small black
eyes scanning the street. "I have nowhere to go. I want to find
some relatives in China. I want to stay. Can you . . . " I stopped,
seeing that his eyes were fixed on my torso. I swallowed hard,
hoping my fears would go down with my bile. I had no choice
but to continue on with my plan. "Could you house me until I
am dry and give me clothes to wear so I will not be recognized?"

The man's Korean was different from my own, the ends of
his sentences tilting up instead of down. He used language that
was very traditional and incorporated words I had never heard
before. But we understood each other well enough. He nodded.
"Come in." He shut the door and handed me a rag to wipe my
feet, which were covered in sand and small pebbles.

"We can help you," he said. He guided me down the long
corridor into a room at the far end of the house where five

women were seated on the floor, their legs folded underneath them. They were from Chosun like me; I could tell by their loose dark clothing, their darkened and dirty faces and their pale, vacant eyes. Koreans in China wore bright-coloured clothing and skirts, pants and tops that were tight-fitting, like Chinese outfits. The women from Chosun greeted me with a slight bow of the head, relaying to me, through their lack of eye contact and slow movements, their hopelessness.

The man who owned the house circled the women slowly. They put down their bowls of rice and lowered their gazes. They seemed afraid of him. I shook off my fears and chalked up my apprehension to his appearance. Blue veins pulsed on the sides of his forehead when he spoke, and he was fat. Everyone in Chosun had shrunk, but this man was even larger than when I first met him, solid, like a walnut tree.

He waved for the other women to leave the room. I waited, standing in the corner, not knowing what to do. "Even if you find your relatives," he said, stepping toward me after everyone had gone, "they will not have enough food for you to take back to your family."

My upper lip began to quiver. My mind raced. "I don't know what else to do," I said, biting my lip to stop myself from crying.

"You could marry a Chinese man," the house owner said, his tone of voice eager. I shivered. He reminded me of a tiger I had once seen while visiting my grandparents in Hoeryong, its breath steaming in the cold midwinter air as it lifted its strong legs in and out of the snow. "Your husband," the man continued, "will help you send money to your family. I can arrange it."

"Marriage." I inserted the word into my heavy thoughts. I had vowed never to let love touch me again after losing Sung-min. But marriage without love? Marriage that would provide my family with food? Marriage that would allow me to keep my own money to clean myself up and to reclaim Sungmin?

"Yes," I said quickly before I could change my mind.

The homeowner curled his lips into a smile. I could smell his sweat. Like the other women from Chosun, I was afraid of this man. I was afraid of what he was proposing. I was afraid he wanted me for himself. I began to feel dizzy but I steadied myself. I wanted the man to see any beauty that remained inside of me, making me deserving of a husband.

THE WOMEN FROM Chosun were surly for the rest of the evening, holding their conversations in whispers. They moved as a group to which I did not belong. Instead, I was placed in the care of a young woman, an ethnic Korean, who wore a tight-fitting red Chinese dress and whose mannerisms were gentle, like a house mouse. She helped me prepare a bed in a darkened room at the back of the house, fetched me a meal of noodles and tofu, and then took me to the stone bathhouse out back to wash.

"Are those women getting married too?" I asked.

The slim woman nodded. I was still wearing my soiled and torn clothes from Chosun. "Don't be shy around me," she said, unbuttoning my shirt. I let her take my clothes off until only my underwear remained. The woman took a sponge and some white soap and began washing my body.

It took three scrubs with a wiry brush and many rinses to remove the mud that had caked in every fold, crevice and line on my body. I had not washed my hair in more than half a year, and strands came out in big handfuls when the young woman massaged oil into my scalp.

When I was finally clean, the woman wrapped a rose-coloured robe covered in tiny violet flowers around me. Once I was seated on a low white stool, she combed out my hair and trimmed the split ends. She then massaged sweet-smelling oil into my feet and legs. "I have new clothes for you, too," she said. "Come with me."

The woman led me back into the house. In another room at the back, she turned on an overhead light. A lime green shirt hung from a peg on the wall. On the floor was a matching pair of pants, along with some white sandals. "Try these things on," she urged.

To my shock, the pants were as short as my underpants. I let out a small scream. I'd never shown so much of my legs in public before. Even as a young schoolgirl, the shortest my skirt had ever come was to my knees.

"There must be some mistake," I mumbled. "Where is the rest of the outfit?"

"There is no more," the young woman said laughing. "This is what women wear in China. Tomorrow he will come. You will wear this outfit when you meet him."

I gasped, wondering how could the homeowner have arranged my marriage so quickly. And how could I let my new husband see me wearing these pants? He would think I was a loose woman. I began to panic.

"Gwangwon is the middleman," the woman explained, seeing my distress. "He is the one who will take you to Beijing. We are selling you to him, and he will then sell you to your husband."

Chapter Nineteen

GWANGWON WAS A slim man, tall in stature with jittery movements. He was dressed in a yellow shirt and form-fitting white pants that accentuated his thin legs. He licked his lips as he inspected me, then paid the owner of the house some Chinese yuan. I wanted to ask them how much. How much was I worth? But I dared not speak as I stood shivering in my skimpy outfit.

We set off that morning in Gwangwon's compact car. The stone houses of Adong were soon swallowed up by the tall pine trees and sloping hills of China's forests. Sitting in the passenger seat, I hugged my knees, self-conscious about Gwangwon seeing my bare legs. With every turn in the road, my body slid toward him.

We said nothing to each other. Gwangwon grunted as he passed me some tofu to eat, and then, later in the day, some rice and chicken. We drove for hours in the lonely countryside dotted with rice fields. I finally fell asleep, waking only when Gwangwon tapped my shoulder and announced: "We're near Beijing." The roads were full of cars. I gasped at them. I had never seen so many automobiles. In Chosun, no one drove anymore. There wasn't any gas.

"Are we near Hadong Orchard?" I asked.

"How do you know of such a place?" he replied, scrunching up his forehead.

"I have family there," I replied, hanging on to my dream of finding my father's family.

"I bet you don't know their names?" he asked sourly. When I didn't reply, he laughed. "Foolish girl, I've met lots like you searching for relatives you don't know. If you have family in Hadong Orchard you will never find them."

My heart was sinking and my eyes grew cloudy with tears as I looked out the window. The sky over Beijing was dark by the time we arrived, but the streets were bright. Red, green, blue and yellow lights hung overhead from large buildings that stretched toward the moon. I tried to stay calm, to show Gwangwon that I was not afraid. People on bikes with engines attached zoomed in and out of the traffic. A few times, a rider with a long-haired woman holding onto him swerved so close to the car I covered my eyes, thinking we would collide. But we didn't.

There were so many brightly dressed people walking and talking in the streets that it reminded me of the days when azaleas would bloom in Hoeryong. Some of the women here wore skirts just as short as my pants, their legs thrust toward the men who circled them. I felt uncomfortable due to their lack of modesty, but also relaxed, since they were dressed like me. Gwangwon opened his window as we drove slowly by.

Eventually he turned down a quiet street full of weeping willow trees and parked outside a cement house. The house was his, he told me as we walked up to the front door.

His wife, also Korean, opened the door before we knocked, bowing and gesturing for me to come in. She wore a tight pale-pink silk dress with red flowers on it.

The house was low and narrow. I could nearly touch the ceilings. I was led into a room and told to sit. Gwangwon's wife brought me a bowl of noodles with pork. The meat was salty and stung my dry lips.

A straw mat and a thin white cotton shirt and pants were already laid out on the floor. I would sleep here, Gwangwon informed me. "We have three men and their families coming tomorrow to look at you," he said. "When you wake in the morning, change back into the outfit you are wearing."

He stepped toward me, alcohol on his breath. He must have been drinking in one of the other rooms while I ate my meal. "Before you leave this house, you will be sleeping with me," he whispered in my ear, his hand moving up to touch my breast. I grimaced and pushed him away. But I knew he might be right. I had no power. He left the room, and I choked back tears as I changed into the loose cotton garments.

I SPENT A sleepless night, and in the morning Gwangwon's wife directed me to the washing room out back. After I had dressed in the short green pants and matching top, she brushed my hair and applied cream and powder to my face. The make-up was a pink colour that matched my skin tone, not white like we wore in Chosun. She used a black pencil around my eyes. "Much better," she said, stepping back to take a look at my dolled-up face. The final touch was pink lipstick, which she applied after first outlining my lips in red pencil.

She held up a mirror to my face when she was done. What I saw startled me. I didn't recognize myself. I had become one of the women I'd seen on the Beijing streets.

The first man to whom I was introduced was old, the age my grandfather would have been if he was still alive. The man arrived with an even older sister, who wore a long flowery gown and a feather in her hair. She sat across from me at a red lacquer table while the old man moved in beside me. One of his legs was so stiff he could not bend it. He stuck it out underneath the table, like a log stretching across the river.

The man started speaking to me in Mandarin. His voice was deep, reminding me of gurgling water. Gwangwon and his wife took turns translating. They told me the man was seventy, with grown children and grandchildren. He owned a factory. He was rich. He would care for me. Soon the old man began a conversation with Gwangwon, who kept shaking his head. The old man eventually pulled himself up using his cane and left with a huff.

I sat quietly waiting for my next suitor. I could hear the wind rattling the shutters and the sound of laughing children outside. Freedom, I thought longingly. Freedom to go home. But then I reminded myself that only starvation waited for me there.

The next man was younger. He was handsome, with a solid build and big round eyes. He smelled of fall leaves and rain. When he turned to me, bowed his head and said something in Mandarin, I nodded, wanting to please him. He seemed kind, sitting with his hands folded peacefully on his knees. This man also owned a factory. He too was rich. But before Gwangwon could finish translating, the man interrupted. He turned to me again and began to speak in Mandarin. This time, his voice sounded like claps of thunder, startling me.

"He will not take you," Gwangwon translated as the man stood up and left. "You don't even know how to say mother or father in Mandarin. He wants someone he can talk to."

Four days passed like this, man after man. I must have seen ten future husbands, all of whom owned factories. Most showed up for our meeting with a female relative: a sister, an aunt, even a mother. But none of them wanted to marry me. Every night, Gwangwon would come to my room begging me to take him into my bed. Every night I sent him away cursing. But I knew if I was not sold soon, the night would come when I would no longer be able to hold him off.

On day five, Gwangwon told me there was only one man left. His name was Wangxiung. Wangxiung sat down close beside me. He slipped his hand underneath the table and started rubbing my bare legs. I tried to pull away, but Gwangwon's wife sat on the other side of me, the weight of her body forcing me to stay in place.

Very little was translated for me this time, other than that this man owned an explosives factory that made fireworks for festivals. "He's very rich," said Gwangwon. He winked. "Very rich."

This time, the bickering back and forth in Mandarin over my price was quick. Wangxiung seemed to agree to Gwangwon's terms. As tea was served, Wangxiung's hand moved farther up my thigh, and he was soon stroking the skin underneath my shorts. I flinched. Frightened, I started to plead with Gwangwon not to go through with the deal. His wife took my hands and folded them on my lap. "Go to this man's house and then run away. That is all you can do," she said to me in Korean, smiling so that my new husband didn't get suspicious. "My husband paid a lot for you. We need the money back from the sale."

I turned and looked coyly at Wangxiung, as Gwangwon's wife had instructed me to do. Then I leaned over the table and whispered to Gwangwon, "If you touch me tonight, I will not go tomorrow." His face twitched, and I waited for an explosion. Instead, he agreed. I discovered that day I did have power. Not a lot, but enough to keep me alive.

THE NEXT DAY, Wangxiung returned to the house with a minivan and driver. I was dressed in a floor-length, white silk dress with tiny flowers on it that Gwangwon's wife had laid out for me that morning. I watched as Wangxiung counted out the money, large bills he unfolded from a small leather wallet and passed to Gwangwon.

It took a full day of travel to get to his home. We stopped only once, for a few hours, so the driver could sleep. Wangxiung sat close to me and fondled me as if I was my niece's doll. I let him touch me, vowing to myself that I would run away after stealing this man's money. Until I could plot my escape, I would be quiet and subservient. Eventually, he fell asleep and I could relax a little.

When we arrived at Wangxiung's village, a collection of brick buildings in a rural setting, my heart sank. People had lined up to meet me. I was on display. As the van stopped, Wangxiung guided me out of the vehicle. People stared at me, some laughing, some curious. No one bowed or greeted me.

Wangxiung's house was small. A long, dark corridor connected a series of rooms. Another woman my age was there. She was Chinese, so I couldn't understand what she said, but we began to communicate right away with our hands, drawing pictures in the air and accentuating them with our facial expressions.

The woman pointed to another man who looked just like Wangxiung, only thinner. A twin brother, I thought. She was his wife, she indicated by crossing her fingers and putting them to her lips. Then she made a sad face. She pointed to her stomach and put her hair up as if in pigtails. A child, I thought. She has a daughter she has left behind.

That night, Wangxiung made me strip naked in front of him. He took my dress and the small bag containing my green outfit and put them away in a cupboard secured with a padlock. I was trapped. A caged animal, I thought to myself.

I pushed all emotion out of my mind so that I was numb. Wangxiung pulled me into his arms so tightly I could barely breathe. His hands touched every place on my body. His foul scent repulsed me. But he didn't try to penetrate me. I realized he couldn't.

Each morning after that, I woke to a house that smelled of chopped onions, peppers and fresh flowers. Wangxiung would choose the dress he wanted me to wear, either a red silk Chinese outfit or one that was navy blue with white flowers painted on the fabric. Both reeked of another woman's perspiration. Wangxiung's brother and wife lived with us, along with the brothers' mother and father. I developed a mantra. "If I do not find a way to escape today, then tomorrow."

Wangxiung didn't own a factory after all. His brother made firecrackers, as Gwangwon had translated, but in their kitchen, with the chemicals stored on the shelves beside the noodles, herbs and spices that were kept in small glass jars. Wangxiung spent his days following me around the house, his arm slung over my shoulder. I couldn't even go to the bathroom without his sister-in-law or mother accompanying me. They would wait outside the outhouse, which was nothing but four slabs of wood over a hole in the ground. Half of the hole was inside the house, the other half outside, so that the pigs on the other side of the wooden planks could eat our feces. The stench was so overwhelming I covered my face with my hands. In Chosun, we would have reported such vulgarity to the Party. But here in this rural village, where the call of a rooster woke me in the morning and the howl of dogs put me to sleep, that was life.

One day after Wangxiung had left the room, his brother's wife, whose name I had learned was Zhiying Huang, pointed to her temple and rolled her eyes. She stuck out her tongue. "The village idiot," I thought. "That is my husband. No wonder everyone came to see me arrive. They wanted to see who would marry such a person!"

Zhiying nodded when she saw that I understood.

Whenever I managed to be alone in the room I shared with Wangxiung, I wept. I was suffocating in this prison. I felt so far away from my goal of finding my family's relatives and then reclaiming Sungmin. One morning when my eyes were puffy from crying and my arms and legs were trembling, Zhiying thought I was sick and served me tea with herbs.

I ran to the kitchen and grabbed a fountain pen and a piece of the rice paper Wangxiung's brother used for his firecrackers. "I can't live in this house anymore," I wrote in Korean. "Please talk to the people of this house. Please help me get back to where I came from."

Zhiying gave my letter to Wangxiung and his brother. They couldn't read it. But they seemed concerned. They took my note and left the house.

Zhiying followed me to the washhouse out back. After she had closed the door, light streaming in through small holes in the wall, she pulled some more rice paper and the fountain pen from the waist of her skirt. For the next hour, we drew stick people to learn each other's stories. It seemed she had been married before and had two children: a girl with pigtails and a boy. I pointed to my chest. "Me too," I said. Next she wrote down some numbers and pointed to me. Three thousand yuan, I eventually figured out. I had been sold to Wangxiung for 3,000 Chinese yuan—350 Canadian dollars. My mouth went dry. That was how much the pig was worth that Myungin had stolen.

Chapter Twenty

TEARS STREAMED DOWN my face, and my hands trembled so much I couldn't lift the teacup to my mouth. Before me stood Wangxiung, his brother, their uncle and some men from the village. The men shook their heads, looks of concern on their faces. There was even a doctor, who gave me some melon and then felt my pulse and forehead.

A man who spoke some Korean asked me what was wrong. By now, Zhiying was also crying. "I'm not sick. I just cannot live here," I sobbed. "I want to go back home."

The man translated my answer for the others. Wangxiung's uncle, a fat man wearing a beige suit on which the buttons had popped, banged his fist on the table and said something in Mandarin.

"They say they paid 3,000 yuan for you. You must stay."

The translator stared at me for a long time. "I know the problem," he said finally, first in Korean and then in Mandarin. "Wangxiung cannot perform his husbandly duties with you. I buy you instead." The man turned to Wangxiung's uncle. "I buy this woman. I will know what to do with her."

"No, no, no," I yelled in a panic, running over to the corner and grabbing a broom. I pointed it toward the translator. "Get away!" I ordered in Korean. At least I belonged to someone who did not want me in that way. Escape would come, I vowed. In the meantime, I would bear Wangxiung.

Wangxiung's family bowed when the translator told them I had agreed to stay. They were so grateful they spent the rest of the afternoon pampering me with teas, fruits, rice dishes and meats. I knew now what I had to do: show Wangxiung affection and loyalty. Eventually, the family would let me go outside, perhaps even beyond the stone wall that surrounded their property.

The next day, I cleaned the room Wangxiung and I shared. When Wangxiung emerged dusty from the barn, I patted him down with a damp cloth, wiped his feet and then made him some rice. I sang him songs I had learned at school. One of those songs Wangxiung and his family also knew, at least the Chinese translation. It was a song about communism.

Over the next week that followed, Wangxiung's mother made me kimchi and a red Chinese dress. Zhiying, using our special sign language, told me it was my wedding dress. Lying to her about my true intentions was the most difficult thing. A knot formed in my throat as I smiled and communicated back to her, "Happy. I am happy to marry Wangxiung."

A WEEK LATER, as Wangxiung's family sat in the main room singing songs and eating pork and chicken, I motioned I had to go to the washroom. I got up, expecting one of the women to accompany me. Neither of them made a move to do so. They finally trusted me to go alone. I could hardly conceal my excitement. Tea-lamps lit the house of heavy wood, and a waning moon cast shadows across the pigsty. On my way back, as I was passing through the kitchen, I glanced over at the front door. Miraculously, the padlock was undone. I slipped off my shoes and socks and crept toward it like one of the barn kittens, ears alert for any sound of creaking floorboards. I opened the door slowly, not wanting the hinges to screech. To my surprise, the padlock on the main gate was also undone.

My heart beat fast as I slipped through the metal opening. I darted into the sugar cane field across the dirt road before putting my sandals back on.

For the next few days, I walked through fields and along dirt roads. I slept on the dry earth under plane trees during the day and waited until the late evening, when I could hear villagers finally making their way to sleep, to move forward. The Chinese woke early. When they did, I would hide myself again. The only food I ate was grass. My muscles ached. But I could not stop. Doing so would mean death. My goal was to find the highway Wangxiung and I had driven on, then follow it back to Beijing. There, I would demand Gwangwon take me back to the border town where he had bought me. I knew he had no reason to do this other than compassion and I wasn't sure he had any. But I had no other options.

As dawn approached on the fifth day, I made my way toward the forest only to be greeted by men's voices. I flung myself down in some long grass and spied on them as they changed the tires on a dusty blue truck. I had seen similar trucks carrying eggs to market on the back roads. Off to the side, a man a little younger than me was leaning against a motorbike and eating some bread.

I crept closer, overcome by my craving for food. I snuck up behind the man and tapped him softly on the back. He turned with a jolt and started yelling at me in Mandarin. When I spoke a few words in Korean, he quieted down. He handed me a piece of paper and a pen, and I wrote the word, "yuan." I flashed my hands, meaning I had no money, then rubbed my stomach.

The man understood. He gave me some of his bread, then helped me onto the back of his bike.

As the bike roared back down the dirt road the way I had come, I started to panic. I grabbed the man's black jacket and closed my eyes, wanting to leap off the bike but afraid I would die if I did so. Into the wind I mumbled the words over and over again: "Please stop. Please stop now. Don't take me back to Wangxiung."

The man did eventually stop, his bike kicking up dust that got stuck in my throat and made me cough. When my eyes could focus, I saw that he had brought us to a small restaurant built from faded planks of wood. He motioned for me to follow him inside.

The man said a few words to a stout Chinese lady, and then I followed him to a secluded section in the back. Immediately, food began arriving: noodles and pork, vegetable dishes and ribs covered in thick syrup. I ate with my hands, which were covered in dirt, leaning over my plate and devouring the food like an animal. The man ate nothing, just sipped on a drink I could smell was alcohol. I ate all the food that was set in front of me. Then when I was finished, the man shut the doors in our section of the restaurant, laid his black jacket on the ground and motioned for me to lie down.

I wish that day could be blocked from my memories. But I was hungry and desperate and alive enough inside that I knew I had to survive. The man saw my reluctance, and he laid twenty yuan on the table. When it was over, he drove me close to where we had met earlier in the day. I hopped off the bike as easily as I had got on.

I LAY HALF-AWAKE under a tree until it got dark. Then I walked all night, slowing only long enough to stuff an ear of overripe corn into my shirt to eat later. I slept all the next day and the next night I came upon a garbage dump, where I sifted through the bags at the top of the pile looking for food. I nibbled on the barest of rib bones and ate some moldy noodles. I even fought with one of the tame dogs to get hold of the bag of rice it was eating.

When I felt the bile moving up my throat, I forced it down. I had to keep the food, rotten as it was, inside me for strength. By the light of the waxing moon, I saw an abandoned sofa, springs popping up through its orange cushions. Fatigue overtook me and I could do nothing but collapse.

The dogs sniffed and licked my face. The bugs that lived in the sofa moved to a moister home, my skin. But I let them. All I was capable of doing was blinking.

The next morning, I made it to the highway. I searched the roadside for signs to Beijing, but I could not read the language. I had passed a small pond, and I decided to head back there and bathe. I rinsed my clothes and hair and then returned to the side of the road, hiding behind some bushes. I watched two Chinese women carrying parasols and big bags flag down a bus. I studied their expressions and tried to make out the words they said to the driver. I pulled out the twenty yuan, and as the sun began to set, I found the courage to step out onto the curb. When I saw a bus come, I stuck my hand in the air, like the women had done, and waved.

When the driver slowed, I pretended I was mute, not wanting to be discovered as an illegal. I pointed to my mouth, then waved the twenty yuan in front of him. He gave me two yuan in return.

On the outskirts of Beijing, the bus was pulled over. Police got on board and started checking all of the men's identification. I sank down in my seat, trying to be invisible. But the police ignored all of the women, waving from the roadside for the driver to continue.

I got off the bus at the main station. From there I wandered for several days, looking for the neighbourhood Gwangwon had taken me to. I slept in the parks at night, making sure I was gone by dawn when men and women came out to exercise. I ate bruised fruit and pieces of bread from garbage bins. I used my remaining yuan to buy some ramen noodles that I ate raw.

I was used to hunger. Chosun had prepared me well for enduring the pain of famine on the streets of Beijing. But one night as I slept under a stone bridge, rain dripping into the gutter, my mind drifted to my childhood. How far I had fallen, how far all of us from the North had fallen. Our gaunt faces and dirty bodies were shadows now, to be used and abused by each other and by the Chinese. Communism, I had been taught as a child, was a system in which people treated each other as equals. Did such a thing really exist however? I began to question it.

Being laughed at by day by children in the parks or spat on by the elderly men playing games, being so desperate that I let a man buy me a meal in exchange for sex . . . that was not communism. Now I understood what Kim Il-sung had fought for. I felt deeply the humiliation of being used, the humiliation of being a shadow.

But what equality had my family and I enjoyed in Chosun? We were treated poorly because my mother's family included members who had fled. My son had been stolen from me, because as a single and divorced mother in Chosun, I was at the bottom of any hierarchy. My son had been taken from me. I wanted to scream, like I had when I watched the tiny flower girl's sister being scalded with hot water. But now I understood why the flower girl had remained so quiet through it all. When you're punched so much that you have to live in the shadows, you end up losing your voice.

Chapter Twenty-one

ON MY FIFTEENTH day of scavenging in Beijing, I saw a wooden house at the top of a hill where people could go to rest and view an artificial lake. I had seen this house through the window of Gwangwon's home. I knew I was close, finally, to finding him.

It was night when I located the place where he lived. I pounded on the heavy veneer door and Gwangwon's wife opened it. She whisked me inside. Her cheeks were flushed and I wondered if she was sick. But she brushed my concerns away when I asked. She led me to the washhouse and began drawing me a bath. "I knew you would leave him," she said, as she took my clothes to burn them in a metal bin in the yard. "I just didn't think you would come back here."

"Can you take me to Adong?" I asked, pouring warm water over my head. The water in the tub had already turned black.

"Do you want us to find you another husband?"

"No."

"What will you do?"

"I have relatives in China, on my father's side. But I don't know their names or what they look like. What can I do?" I stared desperately into her eyes for answers, but none came.

"I need food for my family," I stammered as I began to cry. "Can I work somewhere to make money for food I can take back?"

"I know of no jobs for illegal women from Chosun," she sighed. Her tone of voice reminded me of Youngrahn. I felt the sting of a woman who believed she was better than me but wanted something from me as well.

"I can find you another husband," she said slyly. "A good one. One you can fall in love with. I promise this time."

"Let me go back to Adong first to see the man by the river who bought my puppy," I said. "I want to arrange for some food to be taken back to Chosun for my family." I paused, thinking fast. "If you help me with that, you can do as you wish with me afterwards."

"I'll prepare some dinner for you," she said, smiling coquettishly. "I'll also let Gwangwon know your plans."

GWANGWON'S WIFE TOOK me to the train station the next day, after giving me some new clothes, a tight-fitting burgundy dress with a pair of slacks underneath and matching Chinese slippers. After paying for my ticket, she slipped a hundred yuan into my hand. "The man who sold you in Adong will be there when you arrive. He will take you to his home and organize some food to be sent to your relatives. Then we'll find you a good husband."

I bowed, showing my agreement.

"There is nowhere else for you to go," she warned me. "You realize this is your only choice?"

I nodded.

"Then I trust you won't run away," she said.

As I watched Gwangwon's wife fade into the crowd, I scanned people's faces looking for anyone I thought might be Korean. If I didn't find anyone, my alternate plan was to run away from the train station. But I didn't want to think about that. I refused to live on the streets of Beijing again.

"Are you going to Helong?" I heard a high-pitched voice say in Korean. I looked down and saw a boy of about eight, bowing in front of me.

"Maybe," I replied, looking into the boy's soft round face. A white bandage covered one eye.

"Are you going to Helong?" This time the question came from a woman with honey-brown eyes and hair neatly tied into a bun. She was ethnic Korean, dressed in a sleek-fitting blue silk dress.

"I could be," I replied after greeting her and bowing. Although I had bathed and dressed in new clothes, I felt dirty beside this woman.

"Would you like to sit with us on the train?" she asked. "That is, if you are going to Helong?"

I swallowed hard. "Of course," I said, hiding my nervousness. All I knew about Helong was that it was the main city in the Yanbian prefecture, a region in China inhabited mostly by ethnic Koreans who had lived there since before the revolution. I could only hope that my train ticket to Adong would be accepted.

As her son slept, the woman told me he had injured his eye while playing with a gun. They were on their way back to Helong from Beijing, where the boy had had surgery. "We hope he will regain some of his vision," she said, stroking his hair. At that moment, I longed to hold Sungmin just one more time.

I told this woman, whose name was Eunhee, that I had been sold as a concubine to a Chinese man. "I would be willing to find a new husband," I lied, "as long as he is a good man and treats me well. Maybe you can help? I can't go home yet. I have no food or money, and my parents are dying."

"My brother and my parents need some help around their farm," she said after a minute. "Maybe you can work there for a while."

EUNHEE'S FAMILY HAD a farm outside Helong on which they grew beans, corn and rice and raised pigs. These pigs were well fed on grains and pure ground corn, not feces. It was harvest season, so I went out into the fields at dawn to work alongside Eunhee's younger brother, Jungsoo, who had sad eyes and leathered skin from working under the sun. He was physically strong, determined in his work, and smelled of mud and hay. There was also a gentleness to him. As planting season drew on, we took comfort in the quiet of each other as we worked side by side.

"You do more work in a day than my wife ever did in a week," he said matter-of-factly near the end of the season. It was the first time he had mentioned having a wife.

I was paid a small salary for my work on the farm at the end of each week. I placed the yuan I was given in my shoe. My plan was to pay someone going back to Chosun in mid-summer to deliver white rice to my parents.

Eunhee's family, including her aging mother, embraced me at first. The mother liked having another daughter in the house to tend to the chores. Eunhee was busy caring for her disabled son, whose eyesight had not fully returned. Even Jungsoo's father, who said little and did even less, would nod his approval of my presence.

By the dulling coals of the fire, Jungsoo and I drew closer to each other. As we checked the fields on mild summer days, he slowly opened up to me about his life. His wife had left for Beijing when their son was only a year old. She said she was leaving to find work and earn some money, and then she would return. But she never did. Two years after her departure, she sent a letter to Jungsoo saying she was not coming back. She abandoned their son, Moonjae, a quiet child who had started calling me mother.

As harvest season arrived, Jungsoo asked if I would move into his stone and wood house, located a few metres from his mother's home inside the family compound. I felt safe with him and accepted. Jungsoo even helped me to find a man who would take food to my parents and let my family know I was safe and where I was living.

But Jungsoo's family, who had accepted me for the work I was doing, changed when they saw how close he and I had grown.

"When Moonjae's mother returns, Jungsoo will have to take her back. You will have to leave," Jungsoo's mother would say to me, as we ate our family meals of noodles and pork. "Because of the child, he will need to live with her."

I glanced at Moonjae, who was watching me with pleading eyes. Jungsoo had confided that Moonjae's mother was cold with him, rarely holding him or looking at him with love.

Jungsoo and I didn't love each other, but we could hold each other's sadness. That is what cemented our relationship. I had no status in China, Jungsoo's mother would remind me every time she saw me. Eunhee, who had been so kind to me at first, now informed me that if I had a child with her brother, the Chinese government would not accept it. I risked being deported to Chosun, where the child would be killed.

"There is nothing you can do about that," she explained with a cool air. "If your family had been here before the liberation, things would be different. But now you don't belong here."

WORD SPREAD THAT the Chinese police were raiding houses they suspected of harbouring illegal women from Chosun. Many women, I discovered, had done what I had, left Chosun in search of food and then agreed to marry single ethnic Korean men or be sold to Chinese men to act as their wives. These marriages were not legal. China didn't recognize them so there were never any wedding ceremonies held. Whenever Jungsoo's family's friends came to visit, they would talk about the men in Yanbian prefecture who had taken on wives from Chosun. "These women just showed up and knocked on the men's doors," a squat man named Mandol exclaimed. "The women are dirty and wet from crossing the Tumen River. But they'll do anything because they are so poor and desperate." The friend winked and nudged Jungsoo's arm. "What about the woman you are keeping here?" he asked, as if I was not in the room.

Jungsoo shrugged and looked over at me. I blushed and lowered my head.

"Several of the men in town have made lots of money arranging marriages for these women," Mandol continued. "Did you pay for her? Are you going to sell her?"

Jungsoo shook his head. "How do the police know which houses to go to?" he asked.

"They know who is from Chosun and who isn't," his friend said. "Just look at her." He pointed at me, acknowledging my presence for the first time. "She is so sad. There is no life in that face. But maybe in bed?"

When Jungsoo's son, Moonjae, entered the room, the men switched to talking politics.

In the darkest part of the night, as I lay awake, I would think about Moonjae and feel a string to him that I didn't feel for Jungsoo. I knew I shouldn't let that string tie itself into a knot. Each morning, I would vow to watch over the child as if I were an auntie, nothing more. But when I saw his droopy eyes look up at me with such familiarity and trust, a pain ran through me.

The pain of longing for Sungmin. My thoughts would turn to my own son. I would wonder if he remembered me. In his darkest nights, did he long for me? One day, I hoped I would be reunited with him. I had to believe what the fortune teller had said was true. Sungmin would look for me when he reached military age.

Chapter Twenty-two

JUNGSOO'S FEMALE RELATIVES now played cards and majong while I did all the work, sweeping, preparing the meals and looking after the pigs. For the first time, I understood the pain my mother lived with: marrying a man she liked but perhaps did not love, and then finding herself to be his downfall. Jungsoo reminded me of my own father, stoic and resolute in his conviction that I be cared for. But like my father, he was unable to stand up for me or to demand his family treat me like a daughter. Eunhee had stopped paying me wages for helping with the harvest, so I was now completely dependent on Jungsoo.

The man I paid to take food to my family brought me a gift one month that lifted my spirits: my brother Hyungchul. Hyungchul was now smuggling himself in and out of China regularly, trading goods and food to feed our other brother, our sister and our parents. The situation in Chosun had improved for a while, he told me, but it was worsening again. The Arduous March was moving into its fifth year. People from Chosun were streaming into Helong, taking whatever work they could find and selling whatever they had, including their bodies. Some of the men were getting into fights with their Chinese and ethnic

Korean employers in the fields, where they were forced to work without pay. Migrants from Chosun were being sent back by Chinese police and were imprisoned in Chosun, often for years. At least, I thought to myself, Jungsoo's family had not turned me in. I wanted to believe it was because of my relationship with Moonjae. No one cared for him other than me. I unburdened the family of their guilt.

If only Moonjae was a girl, I heard Jungsoo's mother tell her youngest daughter. "Then we could marry her off."

Jungsoo's friend Mandol had bought a "wife" from Chosun, a skittish woman whose son and father had died from hunger. The woman spoke in whispers when she and Mandol visited Jungsoo, telling me stories of the refugees. The last time I saw her, she confided that she was running away from Mandol to be with a man who was kinder to her. Mandol beat her with a stick, she revealed, rolling up the sleeves of her sweater to show me her wounds. He stuck bottles and sticks inside her and forced her to say things into his ear that made her feel like less than a worm.

"You must leave," she urged me. "Everyone in the Yanbian prefecture is turning on us. You have no friends except the tired man who shares your bed and the boy who lacks confidence even to say his name. They will both turn on you one day. Go inland," she advised, "where there are few people like us."

I didn't listen though, and before long I paid the price.

ON THE EVENING of the twenty-sixth day of the twelfth month, a little more than three years after I had left Chosun, I slipped under the blanket beside Jungsoo after stoking the fire.

My eyes had barely closed when I felt the ground shaking outside. Heavy boots approached, followed by loud knocking on the front and back doors. Moonjae cried out in fear. Jungsoo frantically waved for me to hide in the armoire. But there was no space between the books and the clothes that had been piled in there. I stood shivering in our room in my pyjama shirt and pants, watching through a crack in the door as Jungsoo greeted four policemen.

The largest policeman pushed Jungsoo aside and threw open the door to our room. When our eyes met, he yelled something at Jungsoo in Mandarin.

"Tell him to take his boots off," I shouted to Jungsoo, pointing at the policeman's heavy black military boots. "What a sign of disrespect to enter a woman's house that way!"

I was thinking not of the fate that awaited me but of the disrespect I could not bear for one more minute, from anyone. I started screaming like a crazy woman. The Chinese policeman stepped out of his boots and raised his hands in an attempt to calm my hysteria.

"Get changed," Jungsoo said to me.

"No." I shook my head.

"Please obey. There is nothing I can do."

The Chinese policeman stood watching as I slipped on a pair of cotton pants, two long-sleeved shirts and a man's jacket over my pyjamas. I pulled on a pair of socks, full of holes, and stepped into my one well-worn pair of shoes. The Chinese policeman never took his eyes off of me, preventing me from reaching into the armoire and pulling out my money.

In the other room, Moonjae stood facing the wall, frantically banging his head against the plaster. Jungsoo stepped toward me as the guards tied a rough rope around my hands. "In my socks in the armoire are a hundred yuan," I whispered in his ear. "Use that for Moonjae and celebrate New Year's with him. Bring him some happiness."

THE CHINESE POLICEMEN pushed me into the back of a military jeep. Behind me sat another woman from Chosun, her head lowered. The inside of the cab had filled with the scent of her perfume. I had met a few women from Chosun who had married ethnic Koreans or Chinese men. Some were given good dresses to wear, liquid soap that came in a bottle for their hair, and perfumes from Beijing that smelled like flowers. What I would miss most back in Chosun, I thought to myself, was the cooking oil. At home, oil had always been so expensive that even on holidays we used only a teaspoon of corn oil to cook our vegetables. In China, people doused their food with oil of different kinds.

The jeep stopped next in front of a farmhouse outside of town. The vehicle's headlights beamed on a chicken coop in the front yard and a broken motorbike lying on its side. Three policemen hopped out of the car, leaving me with the woman, the driver, another policeman and a strange man who sat in the front seat. I couldn't see his face but after a moment I recognized his clothing: a large fur hat and coat that made him look like a bear. As I watched the lights come on in the house, I knew another woman would be caught. And I knew now who had informed on us. The man in the fur hat was Mandol.

Mandol was full of hatred, as his wife had told me. Now that she had fled, he no doubt wanted to hurt as many of us as he could for revenge. I watched as the police escorted an entire family—husband, wife, son and a shaking daughter—to the car.

THE CHINESE POLICEMAN who had watched me change yanked me out of the jeep by my hands. The rope, tied so tightly, caused my wrists to bleed as he led me forward. When I screamed from the pain, the Chinese police guard let go of the rope and pushed me along by the shoulder.

My eyes stung from the bright lights in the border police centre. By the time they had adjusted to my new surroundings, I was in a square room, being ordered to stand up against a wall. A photographer snapped my picture. For a moment, I could see nothing but spots.

After that, I was taken to an interrogation room with six other women. We were ordered to line up against the wall. A line of male guards stood in front of us. One who spoke Korean ordered us to strip naked. The women and I looked at each other, uncertain what to do. One woman reached for her shoe and pulled out some Chinese yuan. She waved it at the guard who spoke Korean, saying she would do anything to get out of custody. The guard stepped forward and punched her in the face, sending her flying backwards. She fell to the floor, holding her bloodied mouth, and spat a tooth into her palm. The rest of us slowly took off our shoes, clothes and undergarments until we had nothing on.

The guards moved forward. They lifted our breasts, felt our vaginas, peered into our mouths and ears. I shivered from cold and embarrassment. A woman who was crying had urinated on herself. The guards laughed at her.

The woman who had been hit was forced to stand and undress as well. A guard ordered her to splay her hands on the wall. Then, after donning plastic gloves, he stuck his fist first up her vagina and then into her anus.

My body trembled. I tried to look away.

"Why afraid?" said the guard who spoke Korean. "You've spread your legs for the Chinese lots of times. We are not doing anything you have not done before."

THE GUARDS TOSSED us into a cell no larger than the room I had slept in with Jungsoo. There were so many bodies in there already, people sleeping in seated positions back to back, their heads hanging. Children had soiled themselves as they lay in fetal positions by their parents' sides.

Someone's hand reached for me. It was the first woman who had been in the jeep.

"There are things you need to know," she whispered.

I shook my head, not understanding.

"I've been here in the past," she continued.

I huddled in close and tilted my head.

"When they interrogate you on this side of the border and back in Chosun, you must tell them nothing about how you came to China. Don't say anyone helped you. If you do, you will end up spending more time in jail and be beaten more cruelly. Don't tell them someone arranged a marriage for you. If you must, say you left Chosun for food. They will be kinder to you then."

"What else?" I probed.

"Some of the women have yuan or won hidden in their shoes. They will offer to buy information from you about how you got to China, the people who helped you, the names of your family. Don't tell them anything. They will try to exchange the information for special favours from the guards."

"How long will we be in prison?" I asked nervously.

"A few years."

"Years? How many?" I swallowed hard, hoping I had heard her incorrectly.

"Two or three. And they will be the worst years of your life. But at least there will be freedom at the end of it."

"How do you know all this?" I asked hurriedly as a guard approached the door.

"Because this isn't the first time I have been caught and sent back."

WE REMAINED IN the crowded cell for four days. I sat with my knees pulled up to my chest, sleeping in that position and talking to the woman I called Soohee. That was the name she gave me, though, whether it was her real name or not, I never learned. We stretched a few times a day by standing to do some of the exercises I had seen the Chinese in Beijing do, soothing out muscle cramps and trying to clear our heads of the constant pain and fear.

During my semi-sleepless nights, I had one recurring dream in which I was in a cave, the air so thick with humidity my clothes were soaked. I felt my way outside, following a sliver of light. But when I reached freedom, the sky was dark, full of rain clouds. I saw a faucet and crawled along the ground toward it. I turned the handle and positioned myself to drink. What came out was not water, however, but a jet-black liquid that stained my face and clothes. I would awaken at this point with a jolt and reach for Soohee's hand.

On the fifth day, the Chinese police guard who spoke Korean announced we were being sent back to Chosun.

Part Three

Chapter Twenty-three

AS THE BUS crossed the bridge over the frozen Tumen River into Chosun, all hope left me. People lined the curbs, jeering, "You bastards! Traitors!" as we passed.

As the bus came to a stop, the Chinese border police screamed at us to get off. Once we were on the icy ground, guards from Chosun took over. Their sharp, monotone Korean pierced my heart. They marched us through the main town as villagers followed pelting us with mud, rocks and snow. It was soon apparent, though, that some of the townsfolk weren't as angry as the others. These people searched our faces, whispering strange names. Had we seen their daughters, their sons, their mothers or husbands?

Once we were inside the detention centre, our photos were taken one by one. As in China, we were then subjected to body searches. Chosun guards probed every crevice. One guard's fingers lingered a little longer on my breasts. "Whore," he said, leaning in close. "You are nothing but a whore to the Chinese."

Another guard led me to a cell packed with men, women and children. I could feel through my socks that the floor was warm in a few spots but male prisoners had already occupied those. Other parts of the floor were chipped, revealing the bare earth underneath. I sat down cross-legged in the only space available and closed my eyes.

DAYS SLIPPED INTO nights in the detention centre. We woke each morning at five when the guards entered the cell in their heavy boots screaming at us to wake up. We had to line up to use the washrooms. Many, particularly the children, were unable to wait, so the floor was constantly covered in our urine and excrement. After that, we would spend an hour or so reciting the principles for the establishment of one ideological system. We sat in rows facing the wall where the Ten Commandments, as we called them, were written. We recited them, shouting at the top of our lungs.

1. We must give our all in the struggle to unify the entire society with the revolutionary ideology of the Great Leader Kim Il-sung.
2. We must honour the Great Leader comrade Kim Il-sung with all our loyalty.
3. We must make absolute the authority of the Great Leader comrade Kim Il-sung.
4. We must make the Great Leader comrade Kim Il-sung's revolutionary ideology our faith and make his instructions our creed.
5. We must adhere strictly to the principle of unconditional obedience in carrying out the Great Leader comrade Kim Il-sung's instructions.
6. We must strengthen the entire Party's ideology and willpower and revolutionary unity, centring on the Great Leader comrade Kim Il-sung.

7. We must learn from the Great Leader comrade Kim Il-sung and adopt the communist look, revolutionary work methods and people-oriented work style.

8. We must value the political life we were given by the Great Leader comrade Kim Il-sung, and loyally repay his great political trust and thoughtfulness with heightened political awareness and skill.

9. We must establish strong organizational regulations so that the entire Party, nation and military move as one under the one and only leadership of the Great Leader comrade Kim Il-sung.

10. We must pass down the great achievement of the revolution by the Great Leader comrade Kim Il-sung from generation to generation, inheriting and completing it to the end.

Some prisoners, I discovered, had also been assigned roles as guards. Their job was to watch everyone's lips to make sure we were reciting the commandments properly. If an inmate was caught forgetting a word or falling asleep, he or she would be kicked in the back. Once, my head slumped and I fell briefly into sleep. For that, I was forced to sit on my calves in the corner, my head against the cement wall, my hands tied with shoe-laces behind my back. I had to stay in this position for more than a day.

When the guards were not looking, Soohee and I played a game we called "Food for Words," in which we described the big feasts we dreamed of, everything from tofu fried in salty sauces to rice cakes and plates full of boiled eggs. In my mind's eye, I even saw pork steaming atop the white ceramic bowls of corn rice, which made up my actual meals.

Onsung Jipgyulso was not only a detention centre but a labour camp, and my assigned job was to shovel snow. After the Ten Commandments, I would head outside wearing the same clothes in which I had been captured and begin shovelling, even during blizzards. It was cold enough in our cell. We had no blankets, no mats, nothing but each other to keep us warm. But outside was much worse. I had no mittens, no hat, no extra sweaters. Within two weeks, my right ear had turned red and itchy from frostbite. Soohee and I ripped off part of my shirt, and I tied it around my head to keep the infected ear as warm as I could.

We were allowed to wash every day. But none us were given soap, towels or toilet paper. We all used a piece of our clothing we had torn off for two purposes: to wipe ourselves and to clean our private parts in the icy water we were given. The cell filled with our heavy odours. Our skin was dark and our faces turned gaunt as malnourishment set in. Slowly, we became the skeletons we once were before we left Chosun.

Soohee had been right. There were women in our cell who boasted they had yuan hidden in their socks. Some of them would disappear with the local guards. When they returned hours later, they would sit motionless, staring at the walls, their eyelids blinking slowly. My heart would sink, for I knew what had happened without being told. These women believed if they had sex with the guards they would be set free. Some of them actually were. But most of those women who tempted fate were forced to have sex with as many as ten men in a row, only to resume their lives among the rest of us. A part of them disappeared in their shame and broken spirits.

CHAPTER TWENTY-THREE

The guards didn't need guns. Hope and denial were their weapons.

After a midday meal of more mushed corn, I headed back outside to shovel the snow until the sun began to creep over the forests toward China. Then we headed back inside for more recitations of the Ten Commandments. Dinner was corn soup, then more Ten Commandments, more Ten Commandments, more and more. If anyone fell asleep during the recitations, we would all have to stand up and sing a communist song from our school days.

When the candles that lit the inside of the cell were finally blown out, leaving only a blanket of darkness to cover us, my head would pound with the drumming of the Ten Commandments. I could not escape them. I could not forget them. But worst of all, I could feel no more value in them. We were suffering, all of Chosun. What good was it to learn these rules when we couldn't even feed our children? Even just thinking that, I felt I was a traitor, as the townspeople had jeered. I would shake my thoughts away but they would always return. Kim Il-sung had betrayed us.

My reprieve was sleep. But when it came, I dreamt of the faucet. I would open my eyes to see that the hell of my imagination was the hell I was actually living.

I DID NOT deny my interrogators information, but I did not tell them the whole truth, either. I had originally entered China for food and had not planned to stay, I said. I knew from other prisoners that my family would not be harmed as long as I had not been trafficked or trafficked others into China, so I offered up my true identity and my word that I would not leave Chosun again if I was released. "My mother was sick," I sobbed. "She needed food, or else she would have died. I had to leave."

My interrogator had a mother, too. Perhaps that is why he was moved enough not to torture me the way I had heard he had others. They would arrive back at the cell with bruises around their eyes and bloodied lips.

Being so busy and exhausted during the day, I didn't think about Sungmin. But at night, when the faucet dream woke me, I would spend the hours until morning remembering Sungmin's smiles, his wobbly first steps, his arms stretched out for me. Sometimes I could even sense him close to me, breathing. Part of me even hoped that he had died in a way that was quick and painless, or that he had escaped with his new family and now lived a good life in China or South Korea. Life was not life in Chosun. Not anymore. Moonjae sometimes popped into my mind and I missed him too.

One morning after our recitation of the Ten Commandments, all of the adult prisoners were ordered to shovel snow. As we neared the exit in a single line, a guard informed us that a hundred of us would be leaving the camp. I was one of them, I soon learned. Soohee was another.

Some local guards tied the transferred prisoners together, three by three, and then ordered us to march. We went back through the town the way we had come, shivering in the snow. This time, the townspeople turned their backs on us.

Once we reached the train station, a guard told us what was happening. Some of us would head directly to prisons located near our hometowns or cities. Others were being sent to Kyohwaso, a terrible prison I had heard about from others. Many described being sent there as a death sentence. Soohee, who stood near me, looked over with glazed eyes. "If we get separated," she mouthed, "I will see you back in China."

"Yes," I nodded.

I fixed my eyes on the back of Soohee's head, on her knotted hair, as the train rocked on its journey through the mountains, past boulders the size of houses, gushing rivers, grassy plains that swayed like the ocean. We were given no food. Whenever I had to go to the washroom, the two others tied to me had to come into the stall as well, a guard positioned at the door to make sure we didn't try to escape. My body and head itched with lice. In the warmth of the train compartment, the bugs that had nested in me came alive. But I could only slip my jacket off as far as my shoulders to cool down.

At a stop several hours into the journey, Soohee and the two prisoners tied to her were escorted to the door. She turned, and our eyes met. "I promise," she mouthed the words.

"China. I promise too," I mouthed. And I meant it.

EIGHTY OF US made our way from the train station, our wrists still tied together, through the ice-encrusted streets of Chongjin. Our skin had turned black, our body mass was half what it normally was and our hair was falling out. But the villagers lining the road looked worse than even the worst-looking prisoners in our group. They had no oil left in their skin, and their faces were paper-white, like the origami puppets we had made in school as children. The people of Chongjin moved slowly. They had no energy to look closely to see if one of their own was among us. They were the walking dead. The famine must have hit here hardest.

Chongjin had a large metal manufacturing factory. The sky was black with dark fumes that formed clouds. Soot had settled on the freshly painted white houses with their blue wooden doors and red brick roofs. One thing the government insisted on, no matter how poor the rations: twice a year people had to paint their houses. The soot was like acid, stinging my throat.

As we marched, my anger grew. In such troubled times, why wouldn't the Party let people buy food instead of paint?

We were ordered to a halt in front of a building with two newly painted metal doors. Once inside the prison, more body searches. This time, bugs fell off of us as the guards probed our bodies. Our cell looked much like the previous one, except the floor was not chipped. At least the floor was warm from the heated stones beneath the tiling. The kitchen was close by. Our evening meal was broth with a small leaf of cabbage floating on top. We spent the evening reciting the Ten Commandments.

That night as I drifted off to sleep, I expected the dream of the faucet to return as always. But it didn't. On my first night in Chongjin Jipgyulso, a road came to me in my dream, a road lined with poplar trees. The leaves stretched into a canopy, tempting me to walk as if through a tunnel. I inched forward, feeling the damp yellow soil between my bare toes.

Something at the end of the corridor of trees was beckoning me, though I could not see it. I could only feel it, as a soft, sweet breath that touched my cheek and rustled my hair. The feeling was familiar, like the light of a candle in the window on a frosty winter night. I knew I must keep going. Whatever awaited me at the end of the row of poplar trees was beautiful.

That night, I did not wake panting. I did not wake churning over my memories of Sungmin. This time, I listened to the deep breathing of the other inmates, their coughs and scratching. To survive, I had to stay strong. I had to keep my mind focused. I had to keep my promise to Soohee to see her again in China. I had to stay alive to see Sungmin again.

Chapter Twenty-four

OUR CELL WAS lit by one reddish light bulb hanging on a wire from the ceiling. At Chongjin Jipgyulso, the guards gave us soap, and every morning we could bathe using a pump that brought water to us from deep under the earth. We would stand in our cells, blankets hiding our nakedness from the guards pacing outside the metal bars, and clean off the dirt that was so thick on our bodies when we first arrived it left streak marks on the floor. All of us had lost our pride, but slowly we began to see in each other the paleness of our true skin colour returning.

There was one woman who never washed. I never saw her leave the cell. She was crippled, I thought at first, because she remained in a squat position. Then in whispered conversations, as the female prisoners sat in rows to pick lice from each other's hair, we heard the story of this woman from some long-term inmates.

In a room set off from the kitchen was a big metal tank containing salty water, which the cooks used to marinate the cabbage we found in our broth. This woman, hoping she could escape from the prison at night, hid herself inside the tank, submerging her body except for her nose. But the guards always counted us as we lined up to use the washroom in the mornings and the evenings. They knew the woman was gone, and when they found her, she was beaten so badly her back would never straighten again. She was younger than I was, in her mid-twenties, but she looked like one of the haggard old women who sold rotting eggs in the rural markets.

Exactly what had happened to the woman during the beating by the guards was unknown for she no longer said a word to anyone. But I had an idea to try and get her to clean. Once a week, women prisoners had the cell to ourselves. We stripped off all our clothes to pick lice from each other's bodies. I helped the woman to take off her shirt and pants. It was challenging, because she could not straighten her legs. Everyone gasped when she was finally naked. Where this woman's vagina should have been there was nothing but a black hole.

CHONGJIN JIPGYULSO WAS a labour camp, too. But the city, located on the coast of the east sea, was a major port of entry to all of Chosun. Our jobs were not inside the prison, but at the harbour. Some prisoners unloaded supplies from the ships onto wagons, which would then be taken to the train station. I volunteered to work at the train station, where I would unload boxes of supplies from these wagons and stack them in a room. I assumed this was for storage, until a train came that would take the supplies to the rest of the country. I never opened the boxes, and I could not tell if they contained food. But there was a lot coming into Chosun—boxes upon boxes in ships upon ships every day. I knew better than to ask questions, though I wondered where those supplies were going when the people in Chongjin had so little.

Every few days, at midday, the guards would give me some noodles and kimchi. At night our meals were broth with a few pieces of cabbage. I had vowed to stay alive, inspired by the source of light at the end of the poplar trees, so I forced myself every day to carry more, to move faster, to be as diligent as I could be in stacking the boxes. The guards, pleased with my work, started giving me a little extra kimchi.

In my cell was a woman who did no labour and rarely left the prison. She was already three months pregnant when I arrived, and the father of her child was in the men's cell. But she could not visit him. She cried every night, holding her belly, and screamed with night terrors. She told me that she was afraid the guards would abort her child.

"Surely they wouldn't do anything that vicious!" I exclaimed. "But you're going to lose the child if you do not have better food. A child can't grow on a wilted piece of cabbage and broth." I played the food game with her. We ran our tongues over all the words for foods we longed to taste when we were released.

That night, my dream of the road came again, but this time I was farther down the corridor, amidst the poplar trees. I awoke hopeful, as if a golden light was pulling me forward. In the rays of that light, I realized that survival was far more than just having enough food. Even where there was a bounty of food, like in China, if there was no love, no compassion, there was only death in life. In that dream I came to see that my survival would be based on how much I became one with the others. From that day on, whenever I worked at the train station, I grabbed extra rations of kimchi and hid it in my underwear. I gave it to the pregnant woman when I returned to our cell. I watched her stomach swell. As I started to see life again inside her, life pulsed through me, too.

I encouraged other women who were strong and fit like me to take extra food, to stuff it in their underclothes and give it to the older women in the prison cell who walked with limps or could not see because of cataracts. As if the food we were giving away had become the Chinese foods of our imagination, we all appeared to grow stronger in spirit.

A few times a week, some other women and I were given the task of carrying the heaviest boxes and bags from the port to the train station, many weighing as much as twenty-five kilos. As reward, we were given unprocessed rice. We took twice if not three times as much as we were allotted. We ripped open the seams in our jacket pockets and hid the grains in there. Back in our cell, we used a brick to crack open and remove the heavy casing. Our cell bordered the kitchen, and when the cooks had left, some of us snuck in there to cook the rice. We ate some ourselves, but most we gave away to the weakest among us.

The guards rotated the position of putting each one of us in charge of the cell. Whoever was in charge had to settle the bickering, the name-calling, the hair pulling and the fistfights that erupted and made us forget our bonds with each other.

One such incident involved Sooil, a heavyset woman from a village not far from where I grew up, who had moved to China to marry a Chinese man. She would sit during our lice checks with a straight back and neck and wave her long fingers in the air as she talked. She rattled on nonstop, like a chicken cackling, about how good her husband was, how many pastries and rice cakes she had eaten in China, and how her husband and his sister were so wealthy they had showered her with jewellery, including gold rings and earrings. "Which I swallowed," she said once. "It's all inside my belly. My husband loved me so much," she exclaimed, closing her eyes and wrapping her arms around herself to mimic his affection, "he even gave me jade." I smiled, for I knew this was Sooil's version of the Chinese food game.

"My sister-in-law, the rich one," she announced another time, "lives in Guangzhou." A collective gasp filled the room. I knew she meant the capital city of Guangdong province. I knew Chinese geography because at night Jungsoo had taught me. But I saw some of the younger women wink at each other. They had their own version of a golden light . . . *revenge*.

The next day, Sooil was forced to stand at the front of the cell, beneath the poster of the Ten Commandments. She had to announce her name and tell us that she had committed the most heinous of crimes, though we would not be told what her sin was for another few days. No one knew her betrayer, but betrayed she was. For two days after that, she was made to stand outside in a thin shirt and pants in the shadow of the doorframe, where the wind was strongest and the sun could not penetrate. She was not allowed to speak to anyone. Her teeth chattered, and her skin turned blue.

On the morning of the third day, she was made to stand underneath the Ten Commandments again. The other prisoners interrogated her in much the same fashion as my comrades at school had me during saenghwalchonghwa.

"You have ties to South Korea," spat one of the women.

"Gwangju City, I heard you say," another yelled. "Your sister-in-law lives in South Korea." Fingers were pointed at her. Some of the women spat.

I was pushed to the back of the room as Sooil's attackers hurled insults at her. Sooil sobbed like a baby, saliva dripping down her chin and onto her chest. "Braggart! Arrogant! Cheater! You think you are better than us!"

I yelled too, asking a question, but my voice could not be heard over the women in front.

"I wish the guards would cut you open to find that gold you say you swallowed," a stocky woman with bowlegs yelled.

A hush fell over the room. The prisoners put in charge of settling disputes that day shook their heads. The stocky woman's words went too far, since the guards might actually do what her attackers described. That comment might have condemned one of our own to death, and even those among us who were the most bitter didn't want that crime on their hands.

A tall woman with elegant features spoke up at the same time I did. "Does your sister-in-law live in Gwangju in South Korea or Guangzhou in China?" we asked.

Sooil looked up, her eyes red and swollen. "China," she said, clamping her clammy hands together.

The woman who had revealed Sooil's claim of swallowing gold told the guards she had lied. For her penance, she had to spend one day outside in the cold, exactly as Sooil had done.

In the days that followed, the elegant woman and I began talking. She told me she had been in the Chosun military, something quite rare for a woman. That winter, the elegant woman got into trouble over soap. We were given one bar to share among us. The woman who had been in the military saw another woman slip the tiny bar inside her vagina, stealing it for herself. The military woman accosted the thief, pushing her when she refused to disclose the truth. Eventually, the thief pulled out the bar of soap and gave it to the guard. But the military woman was punished for fighting. Both she and the woman who had stolen the soap had to stand outside our cell, their backs straight, their knees locked, from sun up until sunset for three days. They weren't given food or water.

I felt so sorry for them I didn't eat my lunch at my job. I hid the mushy noodles in my jacket and some kimchi in my pants. When I got to the cell, I dug the food out and gave it to them.

"I will repay you," they said in unison.

"Repay me by living," I replied. "You stay alive, and we will meet again in China."

By the end of one month in prison, I had made more than twenty such pacts with other women.

FEBRUARY 16 WAS Kim Jong-il's birthday. That morning, the women in my cell were partnered and told by the guards to stay out of trouble until we reached our final destination. As we marched to the train station, the woman whose slim wrist was handcuffed to my own whispered to me: "Run when I tell you. When we have a chance, we should try to escape."

"How can we break free from these?" I questioned, rattling the metal that attached our hands.

"With a pin," she said.

"I don't have one." I shook my head.

"I do."

She wore a long, green woollen sock as a scarf. She pulled it off and wrapped it around our handcuffs. Soon I felt her picking the lock.

But the pin did not work and we were still attached when we reached the train station.

The guards pointed at the prisoners, directing each pair to various lines.

"Even if we are handcuffed, let's run away," my partner said under her breath.

I nodded.

As we moved down the platform, I took a good look at the woman tugging me forward. She caught me staring and smiled. She was toothless like so many women in Chosun now.

"Start walking backwards," she said quietly.

We started sliding our feet backwards in unison, as if we had been attached to each other forever. People bumped into us. A few prisoners swore when their faces came flush up against our backs. But we didn't stop until we reached the end of the platform. We paused briefly to scan the station. The guards we could see were all busy directing the other prisoners. We slid our feet backwards again. Then we were outside, where giant droopy snowflakes fell around us.

"Now," she said, spinning me around with such force I lost my balance and stumbled. I jumped up quickly, my arm already sore from where the muscles had torn. But we didn't stop. We walked almost at a run to the end of an alley, turned a corner, then plunged into the crowd on the main street.

Chapter Twenty-five

IT WASN'T LONG before I felt a hand grab the back of my shirt, forcing me to stop.

"You stupid bitches," a man said in a deep gruff voice.

The guard slipped his face in between the other woman's face and mine. "If you're going to run away, do it properly, not with handcuffs on," he added loudly.

He pushed us along, back to the train station, where we were taken to the room where I usually unloaded boxes and bags from the trains. Three other guards joined him. They slapped our faces and then kicked our stomachs, knocking us to the floor. When they stopped, I spat out blood. All four of them escorted us back to the train platform to wait.

"You know, it's Kim Jong-il's birthday," one of the guards said. He was young with full cheeks and innocent eyes, what I imagined Sungmin would look like when he reached military age.

I nodded.

"Something good was going to happen to you today."

"What?" I croaked, my throat dry.

"Due to the generosity of General Kim Jong-il, prisoners like you who entered China for food are being granted amnesty."

Tears of relief filled my eyes. "We're going home?"

"No," the young guard said, shaking his head. His eyes were downcast. It caused him pain to give us this news, I could sense that. "You tried to escape with the handcuffs. The handcuffs are expensive and a crime to steal. You were going home. But now you are going to prison, and you'll be tried and sentenced instead."

I felt a cry rise from deep in my stomach, and I began to cry like a baby.

MY PARTNER AND I were sent to the prison in Yuseon. The town was a mere shadow of what it once had been, I could see as we moved through the streets. It was mid-afternoon when we arrived. The sky was clear, and the setting winter sun illuminated the black of the villagers' faces and their ragged clothes, bare feet and sunken eyes. I searched every face as I walked but recognized no one.

In the days that followed, however, my mother was notified that I was there. She began coming to the prison, though I never saw her. Twice a day, she left me food that the guards passed on to me. I felt terrible when I received bowls of kimchi and corn rice with soy and bean paste, for I knew she was feeding me better than she was feeding herself. I was also eating better than the other prisoners in my cell. The guards told me my mother had bribed them with Chinese cigarettes so she could leave enough food in the mornings to be dispersed to me throughout the day.

The woman I had tried to escape with had nothing to eat. Her family had either not been informed that she was in prison or they didn't care. She never told me her name but after a week in the cell together, she confided that her husband had left her before she moved to China and that her daughter had gone missing. "She was sold to a Chinese man," she said in a dull voice. I began sharing my food with her, some days going with less than half my portion.

One of the guards was nicer than the others, and he let us stand up in our cells for a few minutes every hour he was on duty, so that we could stretch our cramped legs. We were confined to our cells twenty-four hours a day now and it was difficult to lift my legs more than three times in a row.

Sometimes I moved my hands through the air like swallows in flight, the way I had seen the Chinese do in the parks in Beijing.

"I don't think I will ever see her again," the woman told me. "I just hope he is a kind man, the man to whom my daughter was sold. That is my only wish for her."

One day when the more compassionate guard had started his shift, he stuck his head through the bars of our cell. The other three inmates who were there when we arrived had been granted amnesty and released. "Something good is coming to you," the guard said to me, ordering me to stand up and stretch. I was to take another train, he also said.

I knew where I was being sent. My next journey would most certainly be to Jeongeori Kyohwaso, where I would be tried and sentenced. The other prisoners had told me that eventually I would have to pass through there. I would be going alone. But the guard had said something good would come, so I was hopeful I would be granted my own amnesty soon. I smiled at him and bowed to show my gratitude.

"WE CALL THIS place the bathroom," the woman beside me said, her breath so stale it was suffocating.

"Why?" I whispered. At Jeongeori Kyohwaso, I shared my new cell with about fifteen women. Inside the cell, we formed two lines. The newest inmates were ordered to sit by the guards in the front. They sat in the same position we had been forced to maintain all day and all night long at the detention centre in Yuseon staring at the wall.

"Because this is a shit hole," my cellmate said. She smelled of urine. Her feet were black, her toenails missing or broken. Her mouth hung open, and she was breathing heavily, likely from a respiratory illness. She was missing many of her teeth, and those that remained were stained yellow. Her gums were as black as the dirt on her feet. I wondered, looking at her, when I too would begin to come that close to death.

A large urine stain marked the front of her pants. The woman saw me notice it.

"You have to ask to go to the bathroom here," she explained, her eyes flicking to the stall in the corner of the room where there was a toilet. "If the good guard is on duty, we can talk and also use the toilet. If we have a bad guard, he'll say no. So we go in our pants, and then we're beaten when he sees."

"WHEN DID YOU cross?" my interrogator demanded. "Was it morning? Evening? Where did you cross?"

I sat on a metal chair in a small, dark room, across the table from a young officer. He was also a *yehshimwon*, he explained to me, someone who passed judgments on prisoners.

I held my quivering legs steady. "I crossed for food," I repeated. "No one arranged a marriage for me. There were no traffickers involved."

"What about your brother?" he asked. "He has not been seen in months."

I fell silent. I didn't know how to reply. I should have known they would question me about my family. But I wasn't prepared. My mind churned. What if Hyungchul had been caught and had told his interrogators I was married in China? What if he was helping people leave Chosun? What if he was a human trafficker?

"I saw my brother a few times in China," I said cautiously, hoping that if he was in custody, he was telling the same story. "He came for food as well. He was not trafficked, nor has he trafficked anyone."

"He's always back and forth," the officer said. "We want to find him."

My interrogator was healthy and fit. I stared at his thin pink lips.

"Is your brother a trafficker?" he asked again and again, ignoring my answers otherwise.

"No," I repeated. "My brother is simply a petty trader."

On the third day of my interrogation, the officer scribbled a few words onto some papers in front of him. "You know running away with metal handcuffs is a serious offence."

"I know," I said, lowering my eyes.

"You will be sentenced to three years. But consider yourself lucky. In the autumn, a few months from now, is the fiftieth anniversary of the foundation of the Party. You will be released on that day. You will receive amnesty if you are good. Those with sentences of three years or less will be pardoned. Those with sentences of five years will have them reduced to three. Today," he concluded, "is a good day for you."

BACK IN MY cell, I shared my news with the others.

"You are fortunate," said one woman. "A sentence of three years or less means you will avoid going to Kyohwaso. There prisoners are not fed at all. You would be worked to death. You would contract skin diseases and die from diarrhea. It is a death camp."

"Kyohwaso is where they put the human traffickers," another woman added. "And those who are disloyal to the state by trying to defect to the South."

"I was in Kyohwaso," a third woman spoke up. She was older, with bald patches on her head and a rash covering her face and arms.

"Why were you released?" another woman asked.

"I was sentenced to death," she said matter-of-factly, her eyes fixed on the white wall. "I was brought here to be executed."

"My yehshimwon was kind," I said to the woman, trying to console her. "Maybe your yehshimwon will have a kind heart too?"

"There is no such thing," she said, turning an icy stare on me.

Chapter Twenty-six

A FEW WEEKS later, some of the other prisoners and I snuck into the storage room to steal some food. One woman lifted the edge of a dark green blanket in the corner of the room, thinking it covered some rice. We were tucking turnip into our pants when she stifled a scream. We all came running.

In the light streaming in from the open door, we could see that the blanket concealed the body of an elderly man. I had seen the mounds outside on the prison grounds where the guards buried people. Perhaps they were waiting for more bodies to bury together, storing this one near our food.

This man's face was rigid, his body stone. He did not seem human anymore.

Then, with a jolt that shot through my body, I realized I recognized the dead man.

I had met him on one of my journeys into China to trade food. The man walked with a limp, and I was surprised he could keep up with me and the others who were crossing. He was so frail I feared he would collapse. But he made it, his face red, his cheeks puffing as he gasped for air. He wanted to trade some fish for medicine he said was for a grandchild.

I had seen the man again when we were both prisoners at Chongjin Jipgyulso. One morning, when we were both part of a group being marched to the train station, he whispered to me that he had smuggled 2,000 yuan into the labour camp. The guards, he told me, had already found 1,000 yuan and taken it. But he still had the rest, he said, for when he got out. Tears filled my eyes now, thinking that this man had never got what he was so desperately hoping for.

The other prisoners had left the storeroom by now, so I was alone with the body. It struck me, in looking at the man, that the purest part of him had departed. Only the shell he had borrowed to live this life remained. My mind mulled over what happens to us when we die. But my hands, as if acting on their own, searched inside his socks and then his pockets, looking for the 1,000 yuan. But someone else had already taken it.

AS TIME WENT by, those inmates who were strong enough were sent to farms each day to work the land. But my body was too weak from all the sitting, and from sharing so much of my food with others. My legs were crooked, and I walked like the old man had, with a limp, my back hunched over. The welts created on my buttocks by the pressure of my heels had become open sores. The only cellmates who remained with me during the day were the women who had been condemned.

One of the women was only nineteen. She had been sentenced to death for trafficking another woman into China. She usually sat quietly, gazing into her large bowl of wheat rice and vegetables. Inmates who were scheduled to be executed were given extra food.

Another woman I recognized from school, though we had never spoken as students. She and her mother-in-law had also been convicted of human trafficking.

"My husband, who cut lumber, wasn't getting enough food for all of us," my former schoolmate told me. "And there were so many children, orphans turned beggars, streaming into the city from the countryside. They had even less food than we did. So my mother-in-law and I took them to China. We gave them better lives."

"We received three hundred yuan for each child," her mother-in-law added softly. "We sold them to the Chinese, and we bought food with the money."

"What did the Chinese do with them?" I asked.

"Labourers on farms . . . the girls were married, I suppose," my former schoolmate replied. "During the famine, everyone in the city left thinking there was food in the countryside. In the countryside, people left thinking the city dwellers had food."

One afternoon in the hallway outside our cell door, we could hear a heavy object being lifted and then lowered. As it hit the ground, the floor reverberated. Moving them one by one, the guards were carrying the poles that the condemned women would be tied to before being shot. The nineteen-year-old rolled up into a tiny ball and sobbed.

"You did well," I said to my schoolmate after the guards had moved off into the distance. "You saved lives," I told her mother-in-law, wanting them both to go to their deaths without guilt.

My schoolmate nodded. "Many were girls who had been living on the streets," she said. "We were assured they would be married off to good Chinese men, rich men who would support them."

I didn't have the heart to tell her that all marriage brokers made that claim.

"Our interrogator appeared to be kind and understanding," my schoolmate said. "He promised he would request leniency for us if I admitted to selling the street children. I believed him, but he tricked me. When my mother-in-law and I were sentenced to be killed, I cried for a week, but now I have accepted my fate."

"When we die and go to the next life, the guards do not want us to be hungry," her mother-in-law continued. "I receive more food in one sitting here than I have eaten since before our eternal father died. But what use is it to me?"

The old woman with the bald patches and the rash on her face spoke up, directing her words at me. "Promise me, when you go back to China, that you will not be caught again." I nodded as she pinched my arm with her bony fingers. "Will you visit my family when you are released, on the way to your town?" she asked, her eyes searching my own. She held my arm tight, and I could feel the panic move through her.

"Yes," I said, wanting to soothe her in any way I could. "Just tell me where I can find them."

Her grasp loosened a bit as she told me the name of her town and of her son and daughters. "Let them know what happens to us here. Tell them what happened to me, and then encourage them to leave Chosun," she begged. My own hand was shaking as I peeled her fingernails from my skin.

Scratching sounds came from the hallway: the guards were dragging shovels along the cement floor.

"They're digging holes for the poles now," my former schoolmate said. I was amazed at her poise and calm.

"And then they'll dig our graves," said the woman who had asked me to visit her family.

The nineteen-year-old was still crying as the guard opened the cell door and called out her name. Next the guard called for my old schoolmate, her mother-in-law and the older woman. The cell door was held ajar, and the women were ordered to walk out backwards in single file.

When the door had clanked shut, I ran to the small window in our cell and peered out. From there, I could see the women were being directed to a waiting truck. Some heavyset guards picked up the nineteen-year-old and tossed her into the back of the vehicle as if she was a sack of rice. Her hands—all of the women's hands—had been tied behind them with heavy rope. The guards threw my schoolmate and her mother-in-law in next. When all four women were in the truck, guards sitting on top of their prone bodies, the vehicle drove away.

Standing alone at the window, I began to wail. My tears stopped only when I heard gunshots in the distance, each woman shot four times. By the time the other inmates had returned from their farm duties, my suffering had left me with nothing inside except emptiness. I returned to the position the night guard would demand from us as the other prisoners entered the cell.

The condemned women's bowls of uneaten food still sat on the cell floor. The inmates who had been in prison the longest grabbed the bowls for their own and devoured the rice and vegetables that remained.

"DO YOU KNOW what they do with pregnant women here?" one of my cellmates asked me in a hushed tone.

Over the past month, the guards had become less strict. I had overheard some conversations in which they mentioned the president of South Korea visiting Chosun. The south was conceding to Chosun, the guards said. Perhaps because of that imminent victory, which the guards seemed to taste, we were allowed to spend time in our cells lying down now, talking without fear of being beaten as a group.

Nonetheless, talking about pregnancy would not be allowed. I remembered the pregnant woman I had met in the labour camp whose husband was in the next cell.

"No," I replied in a low voice. "I met a woman once who was afraid the guards would make her abort her fetus. But I never imagined that to be true."

"It is true," my cellmate said, a look of horror on her face. "Four women in the last prison where I was were forced to abort their babies. One of the babies was still alive when it came out. It was placed on the cold floor until it died. The mother was hysterical, but the guards didn't care. They put the fetuses in plastic bags and stuck them down the hole in the latrine."

My mouth went dry as I thought about Sungmin. I looked around the cell. How many of these women had lost a child like I had? My heart grew heavy.

The next day when I used the latrine, I looked down the hole and saw pieces of clear plastic poking up through the feces. I shuddered. I remembered the man I had been sold to in China and the pigs in his village that had eaten our waste. My own people were at least cleaner than the Chinese, I had thought at the time. But the famine in Chosun had changed so much. Now, or so I was being told, our feces and our dead babies were shovelled up once a week and taken to the farms to be used as fertilizer.

THE FIFTEENTH DAY of the eighth month was national liberation day. That afternoon, the guards took us outside to sing revolutionary songs. I sat on the lawn with my hands folded in my lap, my legs crossed painfully.

Suddenly, a guard with a bellowing voice began calling out names and ordering the individuals to stand. Jung Sunhwa, he said last.

I rose silently, uncertain what was going on.

"Get your belongings and get out!" he shouted at us. "Do not ever commit your offences again. Through the generosity of our esteemed General, you are free to go."

There was nothing for most of us to take. I left behind the pad I used for menstruation, my toothbrush, my spoon and my coat knowing another prisoner would claim them as her own. With the others, I exited through the big room we had once entered, grabbing a pair of shoes to put on my feet. My own shoes were no longer there. Some other freed inmate had taken them. So I picked a pair of reddish-brown ankle boots with a small heel.

I limped down the dirt road, the sun setting behind me. I breathed in the humid air and listened to the electric whir of the cicadas. Another woman from my cell came up beside me and took my hand. We continued on together. We were free. I squeezed the woman's hand. But so were those who had died, I thought.

"I will go back to China," she said as we climbed over an embankment into a barren field. The trees had been cut down for firewood, the grasses clipped for food.

"So will I," I replied. "But this time, we won't get caught. We'll never return to Chosun."

Chapter Twenty-seven

MY MOTHER WAS speechless when she opened the door to our family home and saw me there.

"Your brother has brought us some white rice and sea cucumbers," she managed to say finally, her voice nearly inaudible. "Come."

She hobbled ahead of me down the hall, her body overtaken with tremors. "Your brother has been feeding us," she called over her shoulder, "but then on his way back from China, he was caught. He's in prison now."

I closed my eyes to fight back the tears. "He'll receive an amnesty like I did," I told myself, trying to be optimistic. I didn't want to imagine Hyungchul enduring what I had.

The walls in the house were grey, paint peeling off the plaster in some places. My parents no longer had the energy to clean; I could see that in my mother's decaying body. I looked around the room. Dust had settled on the few pieces of wooden furniture they owned. The floor coverings bore the marks of footprints, spilled liquids and dead insects.

The odour in the house was thick and suffocating: a mix of years of my father's cigarette smoking and the sickly sweet smell of my mother's demise. As I walked past the room in which my parents' bedding was folded, the ends of the blankets torn and frayed, the smell of her death seemed more pronounced. It is in sleep, after all, that the bridge into tomorrow is found. The span of her bridge was becoming shorter.

The framed photographs of our eternal leader Kim Il-sung and the General Kim Jong-il hung in their usual places on the wall. I approached them slowly. The frames had been dusted, the glass cleaned. The pictures were immaculate inside this house that was falling down.

MY MOTHER SET a bowl of corn rice in front of me at the wooden table. I had not bathed in weeks. Dirt lay deep under my broken fingernails. My mother shuffled over to the container carrying water, dampened a grey cloth, and then sat down next to me. She took one of my hands in her own and began to clean it, the way she had done when I was a small girl.

"I am not proud of myself," she said, lowering her head, her lips trembling. "I haven't always done the right things."

I remained silent, unsure where her words were headed.

"When I was in school, I was very smart," she continued. "I became class representative in my final year. A Party official took notice of me, an official who knew my background. One afternoon, I was given a notice by my teacher to attend a meeting with the official at his office. I was asked to take a certain position in the Party, a secret position, a position I was not allowed to turn down."

My brow furrowed. I had spent my life believing my mother was unable to hold any position within the Party. "Does Father know?" I asked.

"No," my mother said, scrubbing the palm of my hand. "Every month, I had to submit five pages to the Party. Each page had to be about one person in our community who was doing something illegal."

"You were a spy!" I exclaimed.

"Even if I had nothing to report," she sighed, "I had to write something." She paused. "I thought it was time you knew my secret."

My body was stiff with shock. "What did you do?"

"I wrote about your friends," she said. Her eyes drifted away.

"Like the cigarettes?" I asked. I remembered the time I had been at a neighbour's house and seen cartons of Chinese cigarettes piled in the corner. My friend had told me her mother was selling them. Her mother disappeared shortly after that. When she returned, she said that the Party had imprisoned her, accusing her of capitalism.

"Yes," my mother admitted.

"And when I told you Sumi's mother was drying fish and had sea cucumbers and octopus . . . " More memories came flooding back.

"All Sumi's mother had to do was write a letter of contrition," my mother said, her eyes now fixed on mine. "She was taken to the police station and had to give up all the items. But she was safe. No harm came to her. And anyway, she was doing something illegal. She deserved to be . . . "

"Did you have something to do with Daechul?" I blurted, not allowing her to finish.

My mother looked down at her lap.

"What did you get in exchange for your words?"

"Fabric, sometimes, for clothes. Extra food. Sometimes the agent came to the house to pick up my writings. You met him."

"Who?" I demanded, thinking back to the adults I had met in our house as a child.

"You may not remember him," she said. "I told your father

he was a work colleague picking up my school reports. He once smiled at you and gave you a candy."

I thought I remembered the man, but I wasn't sure.

"In the second year of the hunger," my mother went on, "the security agent was promoted to a senior position in another part of the county. His successor asked if I would continue reporting. Everyone, including you, was now doing something illegal. I told him no. I was afraid all my children would go to prison if I pressed on with my duties. I thought they would imprison me for refusing. I was willing to risk that to save you. But they didn't care."

"Why are you telling me this?" I asked.

She put the cloth down and, with a shaking hand, pushed the rice toward me. "At the time, I was doing what I thought was my duty. But now I believe I was wrong."

"What other regrets do you have?" I looked at the food but couldn't eat it, despite the deep hollow of hunger inside of me.

"I'll heat up some water so you can wash all over," she said, ignoring my question.

I watched her pick up a metal container and begin pumping cool well water into it from the faucet on the wall. Anger choked me as the water sloshed in the bottom. It was a long time since I had thought about Sungmin. I had pushed thoughts of him far away, since they pierced me like a knife. Now, however, I wanted my mother to acknowledge my pain and the role she had played in creating it.

I HAD BATHED and was towel drying my hair when my sister arrived at the house. She had brought some salt with her, so we could perform some of the rituals we'd learned as children to cleanse the house of negative spirits. I sprinkled the salt three times over the doorstep, along with some water from the river.

"That will fight off negative energy and the ghosts of ancestors who may still be walking on the earth plane and haunting us," my sister said when we had finished.

Once we were seated at the table, Sunyoung trimmed what she could from my fingernails and toenails. "Wrap the trimmings in newspaper and put them down the latrine," she advised me. "When you do so, make a wish that you will never have to go back to prison again."

I nodded.

"And then eat some raw tofu," she added. "That will ensure that negative events don't repeat themselves."

My father joined us soon afterwards. He had been working in the shed behind the house, where he stored mechanical parts, nuts, bolts and wires he had fished from his factory's garbage bin before retiring. He now made machines and equipment, including ploughs for farming, my mother had told me, trading the items in the rural villages. My father smiled when he saw me. For the first time since I had married Myungin, I felt welcome in his home.

As we talked by candlelight, I learned that my family had not heard from Hyungchul in more than a year. My parents suspected he was in prison and recently their fears had been confirmed by a Party representative. My brother was in Kyohwaso, rumoured to be the worst prison in the country. The news knocked the breath from my body.

AFTER A FEW weeks had gone by, I felt strong enough to accompany my father on his journey to sell a rice grinder he had made. We walked along mountain paths to a town where men from two families fought to see who could offer my father the highest price. In the end, my father chose the offer of a lesser amount of rice and fewer won, letting the grinder go to the man whose family's rice grinder had broken a few months earlier. "I'll make a new one for you for the spring," he promised the man who lost the bidding. "You can manage until then on your old machine. This other family's need is greater."

"Your father's inventions are sought after," the first man's wife said to me as she gave us some water from a jug to drink. "We all save what rice we can, hoping that he'll visit. We would not have survived the hunger or the floods, the ground would not have been tilled as well as it was, had your father not come into our lives."

As we walked back home through the mountains, I looked at my father with a respect I had not experienced before. His breathing was laboured on the steep hills.

"I think underneath your reserve, you care about other people," I said to him.

He waved off my words. "You are not to return China," he said sternly, returning to the father I had always known.

I remained silent, not knowing what to say.

"I can sense what you are planning to do," he continued in his harsh voice. "You are not loyal to our great father."

I felt as if my face had been slapped. For a moment, I had felt warmth in my father's presence. Now, as always, he felt very far away.

I KNEW I couldn't stay in Chosun. My parents had less to eat than ever, now that Hyungchul was in prison and could no longer bring them and my siblings food from China. Staying in their home, I was a burden to them. My sister and my brother, Hyungwoo, lived nearby, but they both had families to feed. I had to return to China and find a way to send my parents rice and vegetables. My father would never accept my decision but I could not abide by his order.

I told no one I was leaving on a fall day when the leaves wove a red and yellow carpet for me to walk on. I departed with nothing but the clothes on my back, heading to the train station at dawn.

I stood on the platform shuffling my feet from side to side, hoping the guards would think I was waiting for a train to take me to work or meeting someone arriving from their night shift. But whenever I noticed the guards looking in another direction, my eyes scanned the station.

After half an hour, a woman of about sixty came toward me. Her body was hunched, her hair was grey and she walked with a limp. She moved up beside me and stood as if she too was waiting for the train.

"Would you like to go to the other side?" she asked, putting her hand over her mouth and pretending to cough.

"Yes," I said quickly, not looking at her, fearing I might alert the guards.

As we left the platform, I took the woman's elbow. She leaned on me as if we were close relatives, perhaps mother and daughter. Her voice was raspy, as if her chest was full of water. I wondered how this old woman was going to get me across to China. A shiver ran through me, thinking this could be a trap.

But once we were well past the station, the woman stopped limping, and her back straightened. She dusted white powder from her hair. "We're going to my house first," she said in a low, strong voice, all traces of her wheeze gone. She now appeared twenty years younger.

"When are we leaving?" I asked.

"In a few days," she said. "There is something I need to take care of first."

The woman's home was dark and damp, heavy with the odour of fried fish. As a human trafficker, she had money to buy bootlegged items, including fish. Sitting on the floor was a young woman with sad eyes who was feeding two young boys. I guessed they were about nine and seven, though it was difficult to tell. The children were thin, dirty-faced, eating their wheat rice with grubby fingers. In the woman's arms was a third child who was wrapped in a cotton sash and suckling on her breast. I wondered if she knew what she was doing, attempting to cross the Tumen River with two children and a baby.

"The boys are going back on the afternoon train," said the trafficker, as if reading my thoughts. "She can't take the children with her to China. They are too young for me to sell."

The room fell quiet, except for the sound of the baby.

When the two boys had finished their meal, a man entered from another room. He and the human trafficker pulled the baby loose from its mother and got the boys into standing positions.

"Give them the money," the trafficker ordered the mother. She handed the boys some won she had wrapped into a tight ball and then some rice cakes for the train.

"We'll take them to the station," the trafficker continued, as one of the boys clutched at his mother's waist whimpering.

"You're going to stay with Halmuni. Mommy will be home soon," the woman said in a weak voice, unable to look directly at her children.

As the trafficker placed the baby in the arms of the older child, the infant began to wail. The cries of the three children grew deafening.

The mother moaned, a sound that came from deep inside her chest and escalated until it exploded. I had never heard such a sound before. Then I remembered Sungmin being ripped from my arms. I must have sounded exactly the same.

When the woman fell to the floor overcome by grief and remorse, I fell with her.

Chapter Twenty-eight

IN THE EARLY afternoon another woman joined us, an elderly lady with grey hair. The trafficker informed the three of us we would be heading out soon. She pointed to a pile of used clothes and told us to pick out whatever we wanted. I took three sweaters full of moth holes and some extra pairs of torn socks. We stuffed the extra clothes and some rice and cabbage in bags made from old shirts and pants.

"If we're caught, do not tell the guards that I am selling you," the trafficker ordered. "All of us could die."

We walked down the main road chatting with one another as if we were old friends on our way to sell items in the local villages. Our conversations were full of make-believe. The trafficker mentioned grandchildren I suspected she was not old enough to have. The older woman seemed to speak honestly about missing her family.

We spoke to one another loudly, boldly, so that anyone could hear. We hoped to throw off any guards we passed by our brazenness. The intimate details of our real lives, we whispered to one another. The elderly woman had two daughters already living in China, she confided, married to Chinese men. As we passed various security posts, the guards walked out to look at us, hands on their rifles. "Hello," we called to them in loud voices as we waved. They shook their heads and sighed. Our ruse was working. They thought us to be dotty.

We had a long walk to reach the part of the river where the trafficker wanted us to cross. Since I had made so many crossings in the past, I gauged that on the other side we would have another long walk to Adong or a similar town. The trafficker planned for us to cross the river at dinnertime, when the guards on both sides would be taking a break. "It will still be daylight," she told us. "But I think we can make it."

My heart beat wildly as we continued along. When we could think of nothing else to gossip about, we sang revolutionary songs and then played a game of tag.

"There will be a valley before we reach the river," the trafficker explained at one point where mountains protected us on both sides. "When we reach that valley, we must walk through it slowly. If we hurry, we could be shot from the mountains by the patrol guards."

The three of us did as she said. I expected with every footstep to hear gunshots and to feel a bullet pierce my back, but we reached the riverbank safely. We removed our shoes, then crept down toward the water.

It was a calm day, and the wind had settled. But while there were no waves, the water was high, coming up to our thighs when we first stepped in. I had never crossed at a place where the river was so deep. We hung on tight to each other's hands as the water reached our armpits. I curled my toes into the slippery earth on the river bottom for added security.

"Send me a rope," I said under my breath. "Send me a rope to take me to the stars." The water rose no higher, as if something was answering my plea.

Within five minutes we had reached the other side. We scurried into some bushes where we lay panting.

I was looking out through the bushes, searching for snipers in the mountain ridges on the Chinese side, when my gaze rested on the trafficker's face. She looked lost.

"You don't know what to do next!" I accused her. "You didn't believe all of us would make it."

The human trafficker averted her eyes. "I've never done this before," she admitted. "The man you met at my house is my husband. He used to take women across. But on his last trip, the women were caught on the Chosun side. He managed to escape but he felt it was too risky for him to make the trip again."

With a confidence I would not have expected, the elderly woman took charge. She led us silently along a path that wove its way through the forest until darkness engulfed us. We crouched low, huddled together and settled into sleep for the next few hours.

Chapter Twenty-nine

AFTER OUR REST, we walked along dirt paths through the forest, slowly finding our way in the dark. When dawn came, we took a break to eat some of our provisions. We bathed and cleaned ourselves as best we could near a stream then we combed out each others' hair. We tried to look as if we were ethnic Koreans who had been born in China. But we knew if we were stopped, we would be in trouble. I was the only one of the group who knew any Mandarin, from my years living in China with Jungsoo.

By the time we reached the nearest bus station, it was about midday. According to the trafficker, we needed to meet our buyer in Helong but an ethnic Korean woman told us the bus had already left. I started to panic.

"We have nowhere to stay here," I said angrily, pulling the trafficker off to the side. "What have you done? You didn't plan properly. You've sentenced us all to death."

"Don't lose yourself." The elderly woman stepped in to calm me, pinching the flesh on the back of my arms.

"I only have enough money for our bus fare, but I have a relative in Helong," the trafficker stammered. "An aunt. We'll take a taxi there. She can pay the taxi when we arrive."

There were taxis all around us. The vehicles were bright yellow on top and green below. Even the cars in China are bright, I thought.

"How much to Helong?" I asked in Mandarin, poking my head inside one of the taxis stopped alongside.

"Two hundred yuan."

"Okay. The person we're meeting in Helong will pay you," I said. I waved for the others to come.

When we reached the outskirts of Helong I shuddered as memories of the night I had been taken from Jungsoo's home came flooding back. I shook my feelings away and focused on watching where we were going. We took a few sides streets, then parked in front of an old concrete building in the centre of town.

The trafficker got out of the car and knocked on a midnight-black door. There was no answer. "Tell the taxi driver that we will have to wait for my aunt to return," she said to me. My chest grew tight. We were sitting out in the open in the midday sun, light shining on us like a patrol guard's torch.

"No," I replied. "Find the money now. We need to hide. Can we go to the buyer and pay the taxi driver with the money you get for us?"

Tears started rolling down the trafficker's cheeks. "I don't have a buyer yet," she admitted. "My husband told me to go to the train station in Helong and said I would find a buyer there. Please tell the taxi driver to wait."

I translated into Mandarin. The driver's already puffy face turned red. He pounded his fat fists on the dashboard. "You pay for this," he screamed at me.

"Yes, yes, yes," I said, bowing my head to show compliance. "Whatever you need, whatever money, we will give you when the aunt comes home."

I relayed the taxi driver's conditions: he wanted more money if he had to wait. The trafficker was sobbing by now and I knew if I stayed any longer with her I risked being caught. I settled my eyes on the woman who had given up her children. She had healthy hair and all her teeth. If she managed to find a nice husband, she would be safe. I suspected the elderly woman's intentions were to run away before she was sold and join her children already in China.

I watched the wind pick up some discarded newspaper from the street. The road was dirty, the gutters full of rotting food and papers. While Chosun was dark from the decay of our own bodies, there was no litter. Everything there was used. Here, people had the luxury to discard things they no longer needed.

"I have to go to the toilet," I told the others.

I headed toward the back of the trafficker's aunt's house, where I suspected there would be an outhouse. After a moment, I felt the light touch of a hand on my shoulder. I stifled a scream as I turned and found myself looking into the desperate eyes of the woman who had lost her children.

"I know what you are doing," she said in a low voice. "I knew if I followed you, you would lead me to safety. I can't go to prison. I will never see my children again."

"I know China," I said hesitantly. "In Chosun, you must pretend you are stupid to survive. In China, it is the opposite. You have to be smart. You have to act as if you have power. You must make choices, and quickly. If you show weakness, you're dead. Come with me if you like, as long as you understand this."

The two of us began zigzagging through the streets, acting like friends. I was afraid the trafficker or the taxi driver might come looking for us, so we stayed off the main streets, ducking behind buildings whenever we saw a yellow and green car coming our way.

"I am Yunhee," the woman told me when we stopped to eat some rice and tofu we found in a garbage dumpster.

"I won't tell you my name," I said. "If you're caught, you may be tortured and forced to reveal it. From now on, don't tell anyone your real name, either."

As dusk settled, I spotted a cross atop the door of a long stone house and pointed it out to Yunhee. "This is where we will stay tonight."

While I was in prison, I had heard some female prisoners talking about the kindness of the Christians they'd met in China. Several had received help from Christian groups. Now my companion and I would find out for ourselves.

Yunhee looked apprehensive. "At school, our teacher taught us that the American missionaries carried crosses like that," she said. "My teacher told us the story of a hospital the Americans had built in another country. On the grounds was an apple orchard. A young boy, a patient at the hospital, crept into the orchard and picked one of the apples. The American missionary who caught him tied the boy to a tree and then burned the word 'thief' into his forehead."

"I've heard stories like that, too," I said. "In one, a boy went to a missionary hospital because he was sick. The hospital removed the child's organs and sold them." I paused, looking into her eyes. "But I don't think that all of what we've been told in Chosun is true."

An older ethnic Korean woman opened the door when we knocked. I didn't need to explain why we were there. She could tell by our appearance. She whisked us inside, leading us along a corridor that smelled of lavender incense and burning candles. In the kitchen, she set some pork and rice in front of us.

"When did you arrive?" she asked as we devoured the food.

"Yesterday," I said, not wanting to give her the entire story.

The woman sat down at the table with us. "What are you going to do in China?"

"We thought we could beg at restaurants for food," I replied quickly, hoping to solicit the woman's pity.

A man entered the room. He stopped when he saw us, then started speaking to me in Korean, asking in a kind voice what we needed. I paused before answering, reflecting on his accent. His sentences were smooth. There were no ups and downs in his inflection as there were in my accent or the accent of ethnic Koreans. I studied his appearance. He had a soft stomach and wore clothes that were tailored, but not close-fitting or colourful. With a start, I realized he must be from South Korea.

As the man sat down with us, I could smell musk. "I'm glad you turned to us for help," he said.

"LOOK FOR THE cross," a female prisoner had whispered to me in one of the prisons. "You can trust these people."

Maybe, I thought to myself now, but it would take more than this man's calming manner to get me to open up. A part of me wondered if he too was already planning to sell us.

"We need money," I told the man.

"I can't give you any money," he said, shaking his head. "But you can stay here for now, and eventually I can help you leave China for a safe place."

I felt my heart race. When the man and woman left to get us some clean clothes, I turned to Yunhee.

"I want you to stay here," I said. "I don't know what this man plans on doing. If you want to trust him, trust him. If your instinct later says to run, then run. But I am going to leave here."

"Where are you going?"

"Somewhere I cannot take you."

"Why?" she cried.

"You're young," I said, "and still have a future. You can take the risk that this man will get you into South Korea. Once you are there, you can never return to Chosun, but maybe you can find a way to smuggle your children out. I can't go far from Chosun. I have something there that will always take me back."

That night, after the Christian man and the woman had turned down the oil lamps and left Yunhee and me to sleep on mats on the floor of the main room, I snuck into the kitchen and stole some fruit and rice. I left quietly through the back door, following a stream until I detoured into some fields. I knew where I was by now. I set off to walk through the mud back to Jungsoo's house.

Chapter Thirty

ONCE I ARRIVED at the farm, I hid in the barn with the pigs I had once fed. I tried to nap, but I kept being awakened by the animals' snores and movements. Eventually I gave up and lay waiting for dawn. I was cold, but I was wearing all three sweaters I had taken from the trafficker's house and I buried myself as best I could in the straw. As the sun broke through the mist, I emerged and knocked on Jungsoo's door.

When I heard stirring inside, I knocked again, this time a little louder.

A woman answered. Her hair was pulled into a tight bun, and she was wearing red lipstick, even at this early hour. I jumped back in shock.

"Who are you?" she yelled, grabbing a broom and pointing the handle at me. I took a nervous step backwards and tripped. I fell to the soggy ground, mud seeping in through my pants.

Jungsoo came running, tripping himself as he pulled on his shoes with one hand. He grabbed a hoe from the porch and raised it as if to hit me, then stopped, recognizing who I was. Moonjae, who had come to the door and now stood between the woman and his father, smiled when he saw me. "Umma!" he called out. "Umma, you came back!"

The woman slapped the child on the back of the head, knocking him to his knees. From that action, I knew who she was. Jungsoo's wife had returned.

Reluctantly, after a signal from her husband, Jungsoo's wife let me inside. "That woman is not your mother," she scolded her son once we were seated on the floor. I shivered in my muddy clothes, avoiding Moonjae's eyes. Jungsoo's wife tapped her long painted fingernails. "That woman is not your mother," she repeated.

"Call me auntie," I whispered to the boy. "Just call me auntie instead."

"You will live with my parents," Jungsoo said finally. He shocked me, for he was looking at his wife as he spoke. He turned to me. "You can live here," he said.

His wife opened her mouth to protest, but Jungsoo put his hand in the air indicating for her to stop.

JUNGSOO'S MOTHER AND father treated his wife like a daughter. It was harvest time, and they fed her large portions of food. She didn't have to work on the farm the way I did. Moonjae continued to call me mother. When he did, his real mother would get angry in front of everyone and slap him hard across the face. Jungsoo and his parents did nothing to stop her. I was a servant on the farm. Nothing more. My former relationship with Jungsoo seemed gone.

That winter, Jungsoo's wife went back to Beijing, vowing she would never return. The family's sow gave birth to twelve piglets. Five froze to death in the chilly frosts of morning but Jungsoo's mother said I could keep the rest for myself if they survived. I moved into the barn to care for them. With numb fingers, I guided the piglets to the sow's nipples to make sure they got their milk. I slept beside them so they were warm at night, keeping them covered in hay. All of the piglets survived.

When spring came, I looked after the twelve ducks Jungsoo owned along with twenty chickens. I planted and watered the tomato plants in the front yard.

I sold the piglets that summer for a high price, and I paid someone to take white rice, vegetables and soybean oil back to my mother. I had returned to sharing Jungsoo's bed and it felt safe to be with him. When the tomatoes were ready, I plucked them off their stems and fed them to Jungsoo and his friends and cousins when they came to visit. Life was good.

One afternoon in December, while Jungsoo was out and Moonjae was doodling on some papers, someone knocked at the door. A policeman, I could see through the window. At first I didn't answer. But he knocked again. He wasn't leaving. I opened the door fearfully. We only exchanged happy holiday greetings in Mandarin as the policeman handed me a calendar. When I closed the door and I heard his footsteps moving away, I said the first prayer of my life. I thanked the heavens I had taken the time to learn Mandarin.

Since Jungsoo was a Chinese citizen, I would never be able to legally marry him. Even if he was no longer with his first wife, China would never recognize our nuptials unless I bought someone else's identity or bribed an official, which his family would not be able to afford or be willing to do for me. Thoughts of my deportation to Chosun loomed large, so I rarely left the farm, and I hid whenever any of Jungsoo's friends came to visit. Then, as the Chinese New Year approached, something changed. I realized that I was pregnant.

"YOU CANNOT KEEP this baby," Jungsoo's mother said to me, hands on her hips, eyes narrowed. My mouth was so dry I was unable to speak. All I could think about was Sungmin.

"How far along are you?" asked Eunhee. She had aged since we first met on the train. Her son's eyesight had never returned, and her own spirit had seemed to die.

"I don't know." My mind raced as I considered my options.

"It costs many yuan to get rid of a young fetus," spat Jungsoo's mother. "More if the baby is further along."

"You must not give birth to that child," Eunhee said, echoing her mother. "You cannot stay in China forever, and when you go, you will have to leave the child here. Jungsoo can't care for him. He has Moonjae already. There are so many abandoned children in China with mothers from over there," she said, tilting her head in the direction of Chosun. "We're not going to be one of those families."

I felt my knees giving out from underneath me. I was about to lose a second child.

"Listen to me," Jungsoo's mother said, grasping my elbow. "You have a good life here. You send food back to your umma. You make Moonjae and Jungsoo happy. We accept you, even though we don't want you. But we will not accept your child. You can leave here tonight and give birth somewhere else. Never come back if you do. Or you can do what we say and abort the baby."

I tossed and turned through the nights that followed, listening to the wind whistling against the windowpanes. By the time I awoke in the mornings, crystal designs adorned the glass. Jungsoo did not speak to me. He didn't want the child either.

"Have you decided?" he asked, breaking his silence on the third day. Before I could answer, he continued, "I had a dream. An ox came into the house—a light brown ox."

I felt tears rise. The ox, I knew, was symbolic of the son I carried inside me, strong, reliable, sturdy.

"But he left. The brown ox came into the house and then left," Jungsoo concluded. "That ox, he was not meant to be."

"I can't do it," I cried, falling to the floor. "I want to keep this baby."

JUNGSOO BECAME LESS and less friendly as his family pressured him to get rid of me. He stopped telling me about his conversations with them, as he once had. "You are not one of us," he said. "You have no right to know."

"I will leave. I will go," I cried one night. I had taken my bedding and crept to the far side of the room, away from him. "You've changed," I sobbed, shaking my head. "You scare me now."

Two days later he apologized, but his bad behaviour returned after a visit with his mother and sister. I had lost my place with him. But he didn't do what his parents said. He couldn't kick me out. Instead, when I was about seven months along, he told me he was going to South Korea to find work.

"How long will you be gone?" I asked.

"Maybe for as long as a year. What will you do?" he asked.

I didn't know how to answer. I wanted Jungsoo to take me with him, but I had no paperwork and no way of leaving China without being caught by the police. "I'll leave here," I said, knowing this was what he wanted to hear. "I won't be a burden to your family."

In the light of the oil lamp, I watched Jungsoo's expressionless face. "I'll give you some yuan," he said. "Whatever you want, as long as you leave."

Jungsoo came into the kitchen the next morning, his hair messy and sleep still in his half-opened eyes. "I had another dream," he said. "I went to the Tumen River fishing. I caught a salmon." He held his shaking hands out in front of him, about two feet apart. "It was so big, the biggest salmon I had ever seen."

"I'm carrying a girl," I said in a hushed tone. Water meant women. The fish was a girl child.

"But I had another dream right afterwards," he said. "Moon-jae was playing with a huge snake, a boa constrictor."

I gasped. A small snake meant a girl. A large snake meant a boy. And a boa meant the child would be in danger.

That next morning, in the space between full sleep and being awake, I had a dream of my own. In it, I gave birth to a daughter, and Jungsoo welcomed me back. In my dream Jungsoo married me, because a daughter would not be so much of a burden to him.

I set off after eating some rice and pork. It was nearing the end of winter but still cold out, so I concealed my pregnancy under stretched wool sweaters, baggy pants and a coat that belonged to Jungsoo.

He gave me five hundred yuan and said goodbye at the door. After leaving the farm, I hid in an alley for most of the day. At mealtime, when I knew the patrol guards would be eating, I retraced my steps through the town to the river. At the river's edge, I stripped down to my underwear. I took one step into the water, and then stopped to listen. I felt as if something was wrong but all I could hear was an owl hooting. "Your mind is playing tricks on you," I told myself.

I waded in farther, clenching my teeth, hoping that the water would remain shallow all the way across.

Eventually, I clawed my way up onto the shore. But as soon as I got my bearings, my scream pierced the night air. I curled up on the rocky ground in a fetal position and sobbed. I was back in Chosun, welcomed by the dim light of a guardhouse casting me in its long shadow. Off to the side was a sentry, smoking a cigarette and waiting for me.

I had been caught.

Chapter Thirty-one

"WHAT DO YOU plan on doing with the baby?" the prison interrogator demanded of me.

I had been back in Onsung Jipgyulso for a few days. The two other women in the interrogation room with me, one seven months pregnant like I was, the other far less along, already knew their babies' fates: abortion.

I closed my eyes tight. I felt like the tiger that wished a rope would fall from the sky and take him away. I didn't want to be the sun or the moon, just the stars in between.

"I've made arrangements," I said finally, making it up as I went. "I've made arrangements for the child to be given away after it's born."

Silence filled the room. I thought the interrogator was going to reach out and slap me. But I held my head high. If my child was going to die, I was going to die with it. That much I did know.

"You two," the interrogator yelled at the other women, "out that door." He pointed to a back exit. "You," he barked at me. "Back to your cell."

THE CELL WAS empty except for two elderly women and a

teenager with the bottom half of her leg missing. I stood by the window and stared out over the barren field. It was a chilly day, the clouds heavy and black. The window was cracked allowing the wind to howl through it.

A shiver ran through me as I felt you, my baby, kick.

I wrapped my arms around my stomach. At that moment, a light snow began to fall. But instead of feeling cold, I felt heat. Taebum, for the first time in a long time, I felt heat move through me.

"*Jjanghago haeddulnal Doraondanda . . .* " I sang softly. "A bright sunny day is to come back."

I didn't move from my position until the other inmates had shuffled in from work. The cell was bursting with prisoners. There were twice as many as when I had first been here. We were boxed in, bumping elbows as we drank our evening soup of mushy corn. China had been cracking down on us, since there were so many women leaving Chosun.

"You may have a lucky day coming," the woman on the other side chimed.

I didn't even know the year, let alone the date, I realized. "Why?" I asked.

"Because I've heard that a group called the United Nations has ordered Chosun to stop killing the babies of inmates. It's putting pressure on the Party to release pregnant women, children and the old." My eyes rested on the elderly women in the cell who were coughing and wheezing. They could not eat their soup. Many inmates were sick with diarrhea.

Nothing changed right away. Over the next two weeks, several women died. I cared for the infirm as best I could. When the workers went out in the mornings, I would stroke the heads of the sick, holding their hands when they moaned, their bodies writhing in pain. I used sanitary pads cleaned with soap and cold water as cold compresses for their foreheads when they had fever. In exchange, I took the soup that the sick women were unable to eat. I could feel my baby growing stronger.

On a day in mid-summer an interrogator informed me stiffly that I would be moved to the collection centre near my family's house. I didn't have time to think about whether this was a positive omen because I came down with the intestinal illness so many other prisoners had. I woke in the middle of the night, soaked in sweat, pain gripping my body. "She's having the baby," a prisoner screamed at the guard pacing back and forth.

"Wake three other inmates and hold her down," he shouted. Four women each took a part of my body, two my legs, the other two my arms. But my water never broke.

"She's not giving birth," one prisoner said. "She's got the sickness."

The pain got worse. I spent hours crouching over the hole in the ground we used for a toilet, but nothing came. I finally made a request of one of my prison mates, who had been detained for a petty crime. She was assigned to prepare our food and so was allowed to leave the prison during the day to get supplies. I handed her one of my pairs of pants. I had been given them by another prisoner when she was released. "Try and get five hundred won for these. Then, with the money, buy me some pills to make me well."

Late the next day, the woman slipped me ten pills.

I took three a day, and within a few days I started to regain my strength. I felt the baby kicking again. I was recovering.

A FEW NIGHTS later, I dreamed of the tunnel of poplar trees again. This time I was farther along the tunnel. The light that was drawing me toward it was brighter. When I woke, though my legs wobbled and I thought I would faint from the rush of blood to my head, I was able to walk. I managed to stay upright as a guard led me to the interrogation room. He directed me to sign some papers, and then he said I could go home.

I felt so faint when the sun hit my eyes, I had to lean against a wall. But I eventually managed, without help, to make it to the front gate. A guard opened it for me, and I walked out and into my mother's arms. She draped a coat around my shoulders and let me lean on her as we moved down the streets.

"Why did they release me?" I asked her once we were on the train.

"I don't know. They just told me to come and get you. The head of the local committee is coming by later. She's been put in charge of watching you. It's Mihwa's mother."

At my parents' house, we ate an evening meal of corn rice and cucumber. My mother did what she always had, giving me much of her portion and taking little for herself. I lay back on my mat and was drifting off to sleep when my mother called for me to sit up. Mihwa's mother had arrived.

"You were released because there are too many prisoners," Mihwa's mother explained, settling into a sitting position on the floor beside me. "You can have the baby at home but Sunhwa, I do not have good news for you. The baby will be killed after it is born."

I clenched my fists in an attempt to contain the anger bubbling up inside of me. I knew my release was too good to be true.

"Sunhwa, a year ago you were sentenced to three years in prison. You were released after nine months on a general amnesty and on your assurance that you would not return to China. You returned, however, so after the baby is born, you will go back to prison to finish your sentence."

"Which prison?" my mother asked. Her eyes were lost, vacant.

"Kyohwaso," Mihwa's mother replied. My mother slumped forward, and my father stood up and started pacing the room. "I have to fulfill my duties," the head of the committee continued. Her eyes bored into mine. "You are under watch. I will be checking in on you."

I nodded to show I understood.

"These are the facts," Mihwa's mother concluded. She shuffled her body right up against mine. "Do something about it," she said so softly, I almost didn't hear.

My body stiffened. I looked at my mother, who shook her head indicating I should not ask questions.

When Mihwa's mother's footsteps had disappeared, my father and mother exchanged glances. My father went into his room, closing the door behind him.

My mother took me by the elbow. "Wash yourself, change into several pairs of pants and tops, and then go to your uncle's house in the mountains," she said.

I gazed into her dark eyes, which were filled with tears.

"Your father and I knew what Mihwa's mother was going to say. He believes you should finish your sentence and fulfill your revolutionary duties. He doesn't want you to keep the baby. But I know now what it is like to lose a child. I know your brother Hyungchul is dead. I can feel it. Go, do whatever you want with your baby, but don't come back here with it, ever."

WHEN I WAS a little girl, my family and I would go to my uncle's house each year at the beginning of planting season and the end of harvest season. We helped him in exchange for corn, rice and cabbage that my mother would place in the cupboard beneath the ground.

I had not been to my mother's brother's house since before I married Myungin, but I knew the way well. My mother made me ten corn pancakes to take with me. I wrapped them in a plastic bag I tied around my waist. I left as the half moon rested over the house and my father's snores filled the room. I hurried along the river path until I reached the mountains. My uncle lived a two-day walk from our home if I went by road and paths. But this time I knew I must follow no path to avoid coming face to face with security. I was terrified of encountering snakes in the long grass and bushes and I sometimes froze in my tracks, listening for the slightest sound that a reptile might be close.

Given my pregnancy, my fatigue and unrelenting hunger, I anticipated it would take me three days to make it. I would have to live on the pancakes and whatever herbs and weeds I could find. I could drink water from the streams.

I passed a few farmers along the way, but by and large I saw no one. I slept for a few hours each day under the trees. On day three, it rained heavily, soaking my clothes and hair and weighing me down even more.

I had to climb one final mountain before descending into the valley that would lead me to my uncle's house. I was suffering from chill. I wanted to curl into a ball and sleep, but I knew I had to keep moving. If I rested now, I would never wake up.

Out of breath, I reached the top and began my descent. I could see seven curves on the way down the mountain. The stream that started as a trickle at the top had become a small waterfall by the time I reached the third curve just before the turn in the path. As I continued, I could hear the water gaining force, crashing against rocks and the riverbank.

By the fourth curve, the stream had turned into a river with rapids. As I started to cross the log that had been stretched over the river as a bridge for villagers, I slipped and fell to a sitting position. The waves splashed high, soaking my body and face. I managed to take off my slippers and tuck them into the waist of my pants. Then, as best I could, I gripped the log with my knees and inched my way across. When my hands met the thick moss on the other side, I pulled myself up on shore and rolled onto my back.

I looked up at the trees, the sun streaming down in between the leaves, listening as my heartbeat slowed. My eyes closed, and I saw the boulevard of poplar trees from my dream and the bright light at the end, beaming down on me. I had no idea what tomorrow held, but I felt I was moving toward somewhere I was meant to be.

The rains had been so heavy that the valley I had to traverse had flooded. The tops of trees poked up from the water. For as far as I could see, a lake stretched before me.

I had heard that pregnant women float well, and I held tight to this belief as I waded in. For as long as the water remained shallow, there were small shrubs I could reach and hold onto. When I felt the bottom slant beneath me and the water deepen, I grasped the branches of a submerged tree. The ground dipped again, the water now coming up to my chin.

"I must stay alive," I repeated, first softly and then in a scream. As the water rose to reach my lips, I ground my teeth. "You will stay alive if you stay calm," I told myself.

Finally I made it safely to the other side. I had no energy left, but I knew I had to find refuge for the night. I pulled off my wet clothes and wrung out the water as best I could with my numb hands and swollen joints. Then I forced my sluggish feet to move, one step after the other, toward a village I could see in between two hills.

At the first door I knocked on, a man answered and spat at me. "Go away," he shouted before slamming the door in my face.

A candle was lit in the front window of the second house. A woman with a ruddy complexion and clear, sparkling eyes opened the door. I thought she was about to invite me in, but instead she too screamed at me: "We don't want people from China here!"

I begged her to stop yelling. "Do you think that in my condition," I asked when she had quieted down, "I would be going back and forth to China?"

The woman's eyes moved to my stomach. "I'm due any day now," I continued. "I am going to my uncle's house to give birth. I will sleep anywhere and be gone as soon as the sun rises."

The woman didn't give me a mat or any food. I ate the last of my pancakes and closed my eyes, lying in the midst of her family's outdoor shoes. I left as soon as I heard the sparrows singing the next morning.

Chapter Thirty-two

MY UNCLE HEEJOON was not home when I arrived that afternoon at the three-room house he shared with two other families. His wife gasped in horror when she saw me. But once she got over the shock, she invited me in and served me what food she could, a bowl of corn rice and kimchi. The family was so poor and the house was so cramped that when Heejoon, his four children, his wife and I put down our mats for the night, we were shoulder to shoulder, much as the inmates had been in prison.

Heejoon sold most of the rice he farmed for nongtaegi. He left first thing in the morning and rarely returned until past midnight. His wife and children survived on a bowl of rice a day and some cabbage or turnip. Now they had me to feed, too. As I grew more and more faint from hunger, barely able some days to roll up my bedding, Heejoon's two eldest daughters sometimes left in the middle of the night to steal food from nearby farms. They would wrap a stalk of corn or a zucchini in the bottom of their shirts and wake me when they got back. I would eat it quietly and quickly, so that Heejoon, his alcoholic snores filling the room, wouldn't wake up and demand the food for himself.

The extra food gave me some energy, and I helped around the house by tending the fires. The kitchen was about a metre lower than the main room. My walk was now a waddle. The baby was so low, sitting in my stomach like a weighted ball, that I felt it would come at any time. But I went days and then weeks past what I had thought was my due date.

Then, one morning, I woke to shooting pain down my left side and across my abdomen. I rolled on the floor, wailing, my limbs tense. Heejoon's daughters leapt up and gathered towels. They prepared to hold me down, but my uncle didn't want them to. "Get out," he ordered me. "There is no room in here for you to give birth." He pulled me by the hands, trying to drag me to the door. My aunt shouted at him to stop and left to find a midwife.

One of my cousins ran outside and laid a coat on the grass. I hobbled my way toward it with my other cousin's help. My aunt returned with two women, one of whom took hold of my legs, the other my arms. But it wasn't necessary. Once I was in the birthing position, the baby came in one big push.

I was elated, sweat pouring off my skin. I waited as the women washed the baby in some well water and cut the umbilical cord with a knife. Then my aunt wrapped the baby in a towel from the house. "It's a boy," she said, placing him on my chest.

My heart sank. I had wanted a girl. I sobbed, not from joy but from defeat.

I couldn't look at the baby at first. But when I finally opened the towel and gazed into his black eyes, warmth engulfed me. I felt a determination rise underneath that warmth, a commitment. As the day unfolded and we lay there together on a blanket of pine needles, Taebum, my son, I vowed that you and I would never be separated.

I REMAINED IN Heejoon's home for a month. There were no clothes for the baby. His diapers were towels that had previously been used to clean dishes and wipe the floor. Anytime he cried, I headed outside, even in the rain. I paced back and forth in between the trees trying to calm him, far away from where anyone could hear him. I didn't want to disturb Heejoon, who was angry that I was there. I took up space and food. He also didn't like it that the baby's father was an ethnic Korean.

I begged my uncle to help me cross the river. "Find someone to marry me off. You can keep all the money, but just get me to China," I pleaded. I was desperate to leave Chosun before anyone from the Party found me and the baby, still alive.

But my uncle didn't know anyone to ask so I had no choice. After a few weeks, I left for my parents' house, travelling back across the flooded valley and the rushing mountain stream with the baby tied onto my back. I was so weak when I arrived that I collapsed on the floor. My mother had to lift the baby onto my stomach so he could nurse.

"I am not going to kill this baby," I cried. My mother sat quietly beside me, her expression vacant.

"Umma," I said, trying to get her attention. "Umma!"

"When you have lost a child, either through death or separation, it is a black stain that never leaves the mind," my mother said slowly, as if in a dream. "Halmuni lived in death itself when she thought she had killed Hyegyung. When she got old, she always returned to the time when Hyegyung was a ghost." After a long pause, she continued.

"I feel in my bones that Hyungchul is dead. And your brother Hyungwoo now goes back and forth into China trying to feed us all. It is only a matter of time . . . " Her words trailed off, but I knew what she wanted to say. It was only a matter of time before Hyungwoo, too, would die in prison.

Mihwa's mother stopped by every three days to check if I had returned, my mother told me. The Party supervisor had also come to the house, demanding that my mother turn me in. So the very night I arrived, I headed to the mountains where my father was farming. Joining him was my only hope.

MY FATHER SPENT most of each spring living on a plot of land on the mountain where he now grew vegetables. He had built a shed there, half of it underground. By the time I arrived, dawn was casting its end-of-summer haze. My father was boiling rice on a small stove. The baby began to cry, and for the first time since I had given birth, I did not try to quiet his wails by placing him on my breast or running into the forest. The plot of land my father was farming was located in the farthest reaches of the mountain. No one could hear us there.

My father greeted me coolly. But he pulled down an extra bowl from a small shelf and began serving me some food. As I ate, he covered the baby with a clean sheet and blanket. I slept for most of the day, waking only when the baby cried to be fed or changed. When my father returned at sunset, he gave me some baby clothes he had received in trade from the farmer tilling the land below us.

As was his way, my father said little to me for the first month I stayed with him on the mountain. He didn't order me to perform my revolutionary duties and return to prison, though, and he didn't shun the baby. Instead, he showed himself to be the man villagers so respected when he travelled in the rural areas selling machines.

"If you are hungry, eat anything you want from the farm—there are cucumbers, turnips and green onions," he had told me on my first evening there. Whenever he went to fetch water from a stream higher up the mountain, he returned with a handful of raspberries, all of which he gave to me. I cooked rice and vegetables for us for dinner, and we passed most evenings in silence, listening to the cicadas.

MY MOTHER CAME to visit in the middle of the harvest season. "I see your son being faced with a tough life," my father said as we sat around our cooking fire. "So I have chosen a name that will give him strength. Taebum is a strong name, a big name."

My mother, her pockets full of garbage, rocks and sticks she had collected along the way, had come to let me know a friend of Hyungchul's had agreed to take me to China.

"Something has been organized for you. It is best we do not know what. But I have been assured you will be safe," she told me. She left the next morning, not wanting to arouse suspicion in Mihwa's mother by being away too long.

One day about a week later, my father didn't go to work. We sat outside the shed together, looking over the fields. After a while, he began to speak.

"Your mother and I are very much apart," he said. "When you were younger, she threatened to leave me many times because of my anger. But she didn't. She knew her life would be no life without a husband. But now she is lost in that mind of hers that lives in the past, as was her own mother in her final years."

My father cleared his throat. "I don't want you to think about us anymore," he continued after a long silence. "You go where you need to go and forget about all of us."

I was too stunned to know how to reply.

"I've made you something," he said. He circled around the back of the shed and emerged with a thick grey plastic bag. "The water will be too cold for the baby so when you were sleeping, I sewed this for you. I tested it in the stream several times. It will not leak. You can put Taebum in it. See?" He showed me how the bag could be tied near the baby's neck. "He can breathe if you do it this way."

"Why?" I asked, my eyes searching his pale expressionless face. "Why are you helping me leave? I thought you didn't want me to go."

"Hyungwoo is never home. His wife has returned with her son to her own parents' house. Your mother is dying. Your other brother is probably dead, but we'll likely never know. Your sister has her own struggles. I have not always been a great man but I want to end my time on earth by doing the right thing. I want you to give Taebum what I failed to help you provide Sungmin. You can't stay close to the border with Chosun waiting for the day you will find Sungmin again. You need to go somewhere where you will be safe."

I bit my lip to stop myself from crying as we sat in silence for a time listening to the sounds of the world around us.

"I have received a message from a farmer in another field that it is time," my father said eventually. "Go back to our house in the middle of the night. Your mother will take you to your brother's friend, and he will take you into China."

I wanted to stay on the farm with my father, comforted by his scent of leaves and fresh air. But I knew I would be discovered if I didn't leave, and Taebum's life was at risk as long as we remained in Chosun. My father's parting words that night were instructions on how to place Taebum in the plastic bag so that he would not slip down and suffocate, but also so his face would not poke out enough for his cries to alert the border guards. My father cleared his throat as his goodbye, and he had returned to sleep by the time I left the hut with my infant son.

THE FOLLOWING NIGHT, with Hyungchul's friend Jaesung, Taebum and I began the journey I had made so often in the past. But this time, some things were different. First, I had my baby who might put us in danger by crying at any time. Also, Jaesung informed me, it was a particularly difficult time to cross.

"It's mushroom season," he said, "and people aren't giving the mushrooms they pick to the government anymore. They are selling them in China. Party guards are cracking down hard on mushroom smugglers, doubling up their forces along the border areas. Guards go high up in the mountains to sit and watch the farmers below and when the smugglers leave the farms, the guards follow them. That's why it is necessary for you to leave now before you are discovered on the mountain with your father."

My goodbye with my mother had been brief. I had taken her bony, cold hands in my own. "Stay alive for five years," I begged her, squeezing her knuckles tight. "I'll find a way either to return by then or to send for you. I won't accept that this is the last time I will see you."

I struggled to keep up with Jaesung, leaning on a stick when my feet felt heavy and pain shot up my legs and spine. The baby slept but as my breathing became more laboured, Taebum stirred. I worried we would not make it up the hill, let alone across the Tumen. But I managed, concealing my pain from Jaesung, to make it to the riverbank.

As I slipped off my shoes in the long reeds, a man came up quickly behind me. He pointed a knife at me with a shaking hand, his eyes red and wild. I stood silent as Jaesung leapt in between us, his hands in the air.

"Lower the knife," he shouted.

The man, wearing torn pants and a dirty button-down top, thrust the knife at Jaesung's face.

"We are not border guards," Jaesung assured him. "We will not hurt you."

The man had a bag around his shoulders, bursting with some kind of food inside. "He's a mushroom dealer," I whispered to Jaesung. "He's as scared of us as we are of him."

"My wife and I are travelling to visit her relatives," Jaesung said to the man. "We've lost our way. Please lower the knife."

"You can't stay here," the man said, still waving his knife in the air. "Guards are everywhere. Down there is better," he said, jolting his head to the east. I could smell the alcohol on his breath. "The water is deeper but safer. We could go together."

"We don't want to cross," Jaesung lied.

"Then I will leave you," the man said, his eyes darting up and down the riverbank. As quickly as he had descended upon us, he was gone, disappearing into the long blades of grass.

"We'll go where he said," Jaesung ordered, motioning for me to follow him back into the forest. After several hours, when the night air was at its calmest, Jaesung said it was time to cross.

I had been nursing Taebum, watching him suckle under the light of the moon. Once he fell asleep, I placed him in the bag the way my father had shown me. I slipped my shoes off and stepped into the river. I felt the baby kick as the cool water sucked at the bottom part of the bag.

The moon was the brightest I had ever seen when crossing. The riverbanks on both sides were fully illuminated. I held my breath, making a fervent wish that Taebum would not wake in the middle of the Tumen River. I could hear Jaesung's worried breathing. He was thinking the same thing. I reached out and took Jaesung's hand, clutching it tight. As we neared the other side, I closed my eyes briefly, hoping we would not be spotted by a border patrol on the Chinese side. My wish was granted. We were pulling ourselves up onto the rocks of the riverbank when the moon slipped behind a cloud, blanketing us in darkness.

Chapter Thirty-three

WE WALKED IN silence for many miles, Taebum sleeping soundly on my back until we reached the first Chinese village. Then he awoke, his weak cries breaking the quiet of the night. I glanced around looking for places to hide. But there was nowhere. The lawns in the village were manicured. There were no trees, shrubs or garbage bins. There were no police cars, though. And since everything was so neat, I guessed that this was an ethnic Korean town, with inhabitants who would be sympathetic. I may have been right since no one came out of their homes seeking the source of the baby's cries.

The three of us made it through the village, the full moon once again shining on us like a spotlight. We reached some farmlands where the Chinese were growing corn. "You must stay close to me," Jaesung whispered as we turned off the main road and onto a path that led up a mountain. "The Chinese farm watchmen abduct women like you to sell. If they discover you, they will separate you from the baby. Even saying that you and I are married will not stop them from taking you, if they are hungry enough for money."

"Where are we headed?" I asked.

"To people in the network who will take you where you need to go. I will contact them once I get you to a safe place in the farms on the mountain. Until then, I am your husband. If anyone asks, we left Chosun together. And do not speak to anyone unless I tell you it is safe to do so."

The Chinese farm watchmen slept in plastic tents. We slipped past them as quietly as we could. By now the sun was rising and my body trembled from fatigue. Taebum began to whimper. I pleaded with Jaesung to let us stop and rest. I was so tired and hungry by then I didn't really care if we made it.

Once we reached a particular tent, he agreed. "This is where you will stay," he said. He cupped his hands together and made a noise that prompted a Chinese farm guard to join us.

"I trust him," Jaesung said to me after speaking some words to the guard in Mandarin. "I've told him you are my wife. This man is a friend."

I AWOKE AFTER a long sleep in the tent with Taebum nestled beside me. The tent flap had been propped open and the cool fall air felt good on my flushed cheeks. The sky outside was a calm blue. My head felt light, and I wanted to fall back onto the ground and sleep some more. But something uneasy stirred inside me.

When Jaesung returned, he was panic-stricken. "Sister," he said in a low voice, "we must flee. This man tells me one of the farmer's guards saw us pass. He believes that guard has now gone into town to negotiate a price for your sale or to turn us in."

I bundled up Taebum and tucked him inside a warm jacket Jaesung had secured for me.

We made our way higher up the mountain until we were deep in the forest and far from farms and tents. Jaesung broke off some pine branches and covered the damp ground with them. I lay down with the sun warming me and slept with Taebum lying on my stomach.

While I was asleep, Jaesung hunted for food. He returned with several small boxes that contained white rice, some potatoes and some kimchi. I devoured everything. "Where did you get this?" I asked Jaesung.

"From an old lady working in the fields," he said.

Taebum was awake by now, lying on his back and curling his hands together. His eyes were still unable to completely focus. "He is so young," I thought. "How can I put him through this?"

Jaesung's words broke into my thoughts. "I have made contact with the man who will take you on from here. I've brought many people to him."

"Are you sure he will keep us together?"

"Your baby may be the youngest person who has ever made this journey," Jaesung said. "But I believe you can trust this man."

CHANGSOO, AN ETHNIC Korean, had a round, pleasant face. He lived in a hut similar to my father's. At the end of the day, Jaesung and I said goodbye. He wished me luck as he handed me some yuan.

"Where did you get this?" I asked.

"Your father had me sell two machines to pay me. This is the amount remaining." I was well fed over the next few days, and Changsoo gave me clean clothes that he said belonged to his wife. I was forbidden to leave the tent in case anyone saw me, and my body ached from the lack of activity. I was anxious to get moving.

Finally, Changsoo announced Taebum and I would be leaving that night.

CHAPTER THIRTY-THREE

"No one has told me where I am going," I said hesitantly. "Do you know?"

"You're going to South Korea. That is what we have arranged," he said matter-of-factly.

The news shocked me so much I could do nothing at first but stare at him. I had assumed I was being taken far inland, away from the border where I would be in danger, where I would then be sold. I didn't expect this.

"When you get to South Korea," he continued, "you will be given money by the government. You will owe some of that to the human smugglers and someone will find you there to collect the money. You and the baby will be safe once we get you out of China."

That evening, a tall, slim ethnic Korean man with quick movements arrived at Changsoo's house after dark. There was a Chinese police car waiting for us at the bottom of the mountain, the man told me.

"I will not reveal much about our plan," the man said. "But this you need to know. You will appear to be a prisoner in the back of the police chief's car. With a baby, you are unable to walk the underground network we usually use to help people escape the checkpoints. The only way to get you to our destination is by car, acting as if you are a defector we are taking to jail. A Chinese policeman I have paid will accompany us."

Changsoo spoke kindly, seeing that I was numb with terror. "Don't ask any questions," he advised, handing me some apples for the journey. "It is best for your safety that you know as little as possible."

WE DROVE IN silence for several hours. As I nursed Taebum, I looked out the window at the flickering lights of a town and then the empty fields bathed in the gentle glow of the crescent moon. Each time we reached a checkpoint, the driver spoke to the Chinese guard who poked his head into the car and shone a flashlight in my face. Each time we were waved through. My nerves were so shattered, I felt I was suffocating with fear.

At Hwaryong, the policeman parked the car. The ethnic Korean man turned to me and explained that our cover story had changed. From here on, he was my husband, Taebum our son, and we were ethnic Koreans living in Helong. The name I should use for him was Bongchun, he told me.

Once we'd climbed out of the car, Bongchun hurried me along the street by the elbow, propelling us toward the bus station. Our story was that I was sick and he was taking me to a doctor in a far-off city who was a family friend. "I have a fake document that states you are my wife and ethnic Korean," he explained. "Just don't talk to anyone."

We disembarked in a strange city several hours later, after undergoing two police checks along the way. For the next four days, Taebum and I were locked in an apartment bedroom. I saw my human smuggler only once each day, when he brought me food. One afternoon, he gave me some Chinese dumplings and some clean clothes to wear.

Through the door, I could hear the man making many phone calls. He spoke Russian at one point, a language I recognized from school. "It will be cold where you are going," he told me on the fourth afternoon. He brought me more clothes to layer underneath my own and some extra pieces to pack in a bottari small enough that I could carry it along with Taebum. He also gave me some cloth diapers and a blanket.

Despite the warning not to ask questions, I was desperate to find out what I could.

"On the phone," I said, "I heard you speaking Russian. Aren't we going to South Korea?"

"Mongolia." He smiled for the first time, a crooked grin revealing a missing front tooth. "From Mongolia you will go to South Korea. Now, don't ask me anymore."

THAT NIGHT WE boarded another bus, pretending again to be husband and wife. The man played the part well, taking my hand and holding it, stroking my leg when guards at the checkpoints walked up to us.

"I'm taking my sick wife to a friend who is a doctor," he explained to them. The checkpoint officer eyed us up and down, then handed the fake papers back to the man.

We changed buses twice. On the third bus, I scanned the faces of the passengers and saw that there were others from Chosun. When we passed through checkpoints, I saw them also give the guards papers that said they were legal. I had started to sweat, despite the cool air. Taebum had become agitated, perhaps picking up on my fears. I settled him by singing softly into his ear the song I remembered from *The Flower Girl*:

"Every spring the hills and fields bloom with beautiful flowers, but we have no country, no spring, When will flowers bloom in our hearts, on the hill path Brother was dragged along? Spring comes and flowers bloom every year."

WE GOT OFF at a busy bus station. Bongchun led me to a pickup truck at the back of a nearby parking lot. By now, the others from Chosun who had been on the bus—a woman with a teenaged son and daughter and an older man—had joined us. Bongchun handed some yuan to an ethnic Korean man with black-rimmed glasses and beady eyes, then gestured for the others to climb into the back of the truck underneath a tarp. "You get in the front," Bongchun ordered me. "And goodbye. I am leaving you now."

He turned and left before I could even thank him.

The main cab was warm. I huddled close to the steamed-up window, holding Taebum in my arms. The new smuggler got in beside me. Without a word, he started the engine and began backing out of the lot.

Once we'd left the city, we drove for hours across naked earth. I watched the wind blow loose grass across the wrinkled mud.

"I'm going to drive you as close as I can to the fence," the smuggler said finally. "Then you'll need to climb over on your own. I won't be coming with you."

He handed me a piece of paper with writing on it. "It is written in Mongolian, Russian and Korean," he explained when he saw my confusion. "The others have a paper like this too. Give it to a Mongolian guard once you've climbed the fence, and make sure he reads it."

I hurriedly tucked the piece of paper inside my shirt. I felt faint and short of breath. It was really happening. I was leaving everything behind.

WE STOPPED AT the edge of a field. A barbed wire fence was small on the horizon but shining in the moonlight. "You are in between border checkpoints," the smuggler told us as we gathered around him. "Each patrol is about a hundred *li* away," he warned. "If you see lights of any kind, it will be guards. You must run as fast as you can on this side, and then on the other side, until you see a Mongolian border guard."

There was no time to think. The woman's teenaged son began running before the smuggler had even finished speaking. The daughter and her mother were close behind him. The old man, carrying a large tapestry bag, remained beside me.

The shoes I had been given to wear had small wedged heels. After we had run a few metres in the open field, I tripped. I kicked both shoes off. Taebum was crying by now, and I continued moving as quickly as I could, half limping from the rocks digging into the soles of my feet. The old man had pulled ahead.

From the corner of my eye, I saw flashing lights. A car was moving toward us fast. Suddenly, the fence was right in front of me. The woman and her teenagers were already on the other side. The old man had made it over, too, and as the headlights neared, he lifted the bottom of the fence enough so I could throw the bottari full of clothes and diapers underneath. I slid Taebum to the man as well. The space was not big enough for me, though, so I had to climb. The barbed wire at the top of the fence ripped into my clothes and skin. By the time I had reached the other side, blood seeped through the fabric and gushed from the palms of my hands. But there was no stopping.

I jumped down the rest of the way and grabbed Taebum. He was wailing by now, and as I ran, I braced myself to be shot in the back. But it was dark, and the Chinese gunshots missed us all. Taebum kept screaming, but I forced myself on until I had reached the others. Then I fell to my knees, heaving from lack of air and cramps in my abdomen. After a minute, a spotlight was trained on my companions and me by two men in uniforms sitting atop midnight-coloured horses. The others were holding up the signs the human smuggler had given us.

One of the uniformed men dismounted.

"Come with us," he said in choppy Mandarin.

As the guard helped me to my feet, Taebum's crying stopped. With shaking hands, I pulled the paper the smuggler had given me out of my shirt pocket and held it high in front of me.

The uniformed man shone his torch on my sign.

"You're safe now," he said to me. Turning to the others, he repeated his statement. "You are all safe now."

We walked to the border guards' office, but we were not imprisoned there. We were given steaming hot cups of tea, and a uniformed man handed me some shoes to wear. The Mongolian border guards were kind. One even helped me wrap Taebum in a clean blanket.

When we were seated again, I took out the piece of paper the smuggler had given me and read it myself for the first time. As I did so, tears welled up in my eyes.

"We are from North Korea," it said. "Do not send us back to China. Contact the South Korean embassy immediately. Tell them we are escaping North Korea and wish to seek asylum there."

Epilogue

ONCE WE HAD safely arrived in Mongolia, the group of us from Chosun were taken to an apartment, then to a small house, and finally to a hotel in the city of Ulaanbaatar. We spent a month there, having long interviews with a representative from the South Korean government. Taebum, you were the youngest among us. I told the South Korean representative much of the story I've told you in these pages, to prove I was who I said I was.

Not a day goes by when I do not think about my mother, a woman of spirit who loved to sing and dance. In my mind's eye, I see her as a young woman in the hills full of deulgukhwa blossoms, telling me her stories of lost love and pain. I remember my father as the quiet man who did not how to express love very well, but who I realize now always loved his family. I see him also as the man who made machines for people who had none and who designed the plastic bag that carried you, my son, to safety.

I remember Hyungchul, Hyungwoo and my sister, Sunyoung; the games we played as children and the way our lives overlapped as we grew older. And, of course, I think of Sungmin. Maybe he'll read these words one day, recognize his own story and come to this new country to find us.

I couldn't keep my word to my mother—I didn't return to her after five years. I couldn't risk the safety of my family by trying to smuggle myself back into Chosun. My son Taebum and I lived in South Korea until 2008, when we immigrated to Canada. I am now a Canadian resident, granted permanent status on humanitarian and compassionate grounds. Taebum has since been joined by a younger brother who was born in Canada.

I have learned that my father is now dead. I am uncertain whether my mother, younger brother and sister are still alive. I have never had word about the fate of my brother Hyungchul.

It is a comfort to visit these family members in my dreams. Their faces shine from the end of the road of poplar trees. I may never see them again, and you may never meet them, Taebum, but they are with us all the time. It was their spirits that drove us forward, and with their assistance, we have survived.

Acknowledgements

OUR HEARTFELT THANKS to Soohyun Nam, refugee lawyer and classical cellist, who for more than a year, sat between us nearly every Saturday morning. While Lucia actually started a diary after escaping to Mongolia, it was not used in the creation of this book. Soohyun translated Susan's questions and Lucia's responses, which culminated in this life story.

Soohyun offered her services with an unwavering commitment to raising awareness about the plight of North Korean women and children, with no expectation of compensation.

—Lucia Jang and Susan McClelland

Translator's Note

I FIRST ENCOUNTERED Lucia Jang's story in the summer of 2010 while assisting with her application to obtain permanent refuge status in Canada. Although I had become well aware of the plight of North Koreans, Ms. Jang's narrative struck me deeply with the sheer determination with which she had sought a life of freedom for her son and herself. Ms. Jang was therefore the first person I thought of when HanVoice asked for my help to connect with someone who might be interested in telling his or her story for a proposed book from Douglas & McIntyre about a North Korean refugee in Canada.

Ms. Jang, Susan and I first began to meet in the summer of 2011, and despite Ms. Jang's wonderful spirit and sense of humour, it was difficult to hear the painful details of her past. Having since met and worked with many more women in similar circumstances, and learning that such experiences can remain a permanent source of grief, shame and regret, I have come to appreciate Ms. Jang's courage in telling her story publicly even more. I have also come to discover that the heartbreaking experiences Ms. Jang has had to endure are, rather than being one person's uniquely dramatic life story, representative of an almost unanimously common experience among the numerous women who have fled North Korea.

Ms. Jang has, however, found a life for herself and her children that is free and secure, as have others who have survived their incredible journey. In this way, this book is for all those with a personal story of pain and tenacity. I hope that this story can serve as a record of, and a tribute to, the untold stories of numerous North Koreans who have attempted and continue to attempt escape to freedom, so that their lives and struggles do not go unaccounted. Even when there seems little that we can do, recognizing their struggle and their right to life is a positive first step.

Ms. Jang and I are also thankful to Ms. Catherine Bruce, Ms. Jang's immigration lawyer, who was the first person to listen to Ms. Jang's story and whose work brought it to light.

It has been my privilege to take a small part in the telling of Ms. Jang's story. I hope it can go on to achieve much in bringing forth the story of North Korean women to the world.

—Soohyun Nam, 2014

SOOHYUN NAM IS an immigration and refugee lawyer in Toronto, Canada. Since 2007, Soohyun has worked with North Korean refugees and North Korean human rights issues through NGO advocacy, journalism, law and music. Soohyun has served on the Board of Directors of HanVoice, a Canadian advocacy organization for North Korean refugee and human rights issues, and has reported on North Koreans in Canada and Canadian advocacy efforts for North Korean human rights and refugee issues for Radio Free Asia.

Afterword: Bearing Witness

Stephan Haggard

THE APPEAL OF this affecting memoir stems in large part from its simple humanity. Some of the memories of childhood that Lucia Jang recounts are those that any adult might remember: the joys of experiencing play, family and young love; the anxieties of grumpy and demanding grandparents, lost brothers, playground slights. And we are struck, too, by familiar stories of early adulthood: memories of courting, the uncertainties of early marriage, the challenges of entering the workforce, the demands of becoming a parent. Given the charged nature of the geopolitics of the Korean peninsula, it is important to keep this common humanity in mind; it undergirds our hopes that North Koreans will someday enjoy the basic human rights they have been denied for so long.

Layered on top of this very human story are insights into a common Korean culture. We see the continuing power of Confucian ideals of familial fealty: the patriarchy—but with powerful and enduring women, respect for elders and, despite the Communist setting, worship of ancestors. We see the same resulting tensions that emerge in all such traditional cultures (and that have been themes in post-war South Korean

281

literature): family provides protection and support, but it also demands sacrifices and places particular demands on young women seeking independence, equality and dignity.

Yet the power of this account rests not on revealing these insights but on underscoring the oppressive constraints of the Kim family regime, a silent but enduring and all-pervasive presence in the life story of every North Korean. The dynastic government that rules North Korea manages to be simultaneously omnipresent and distant, pervasively watchful and intrusive yet fatally unresponsive to the basic needs of its subjects. Were Lucia Jang's account idiosyncratic, we would find it unimaginable, fantastic. But through refugee testimony, surveys and outside research on North Korean history and political economy, we have a larger picture that gives credence to every crucial element in this harrowing memoir.[1]

A pervasive theme in this book is continual insecurity with respect to food. What is striking is that this deprivation of the most basic of needs emerges not just during the great famine of the mid-1990s (the period euphemistically known as the Arduous March and described in Part II) when 600,000 to a million people, or 3 to 5 per cent of the population, died. Rather, it is a

---

1 See, for example, Kang Chol-hwan, *The Aquariums of Pyongyang: Ten Years in the North Korean Gulag* (Basic Books, 2001); Stephan Haggard and Marcus Noland, *The North Korean Refugee Crisis: Human Rights and International Response* (The Committee for Human Rights in North Korea, 2006); Stephan Haggard and Marcus Noland, *Famine in North Korea: Markets, Aid and Reform* (Columbia University Press, 2007); Barbara Demick, *Nothing to Envy: Ordinary Lives in North Korea* (Spiegel and Grau, 2009); Lee Hae Yong, *Lives for Sale: Personal Accounts of Women Fleeing North Korea to China* (The Committee for Human Rights in North Korea, 2009); Stephan Haggard and Marcus Noland, *Witness to Transformation: Refugee Insights into North Korea* (Peterson Institute for International Economics, 2011); Melanie Kirkpatrick, *Escape from North Korea: The Untold Story of Asia's Underground Railroad* (Encounter Books, 2012); Robert Collins, *Marked for Life: Songbun, North Korea's Social Classification System* (The Committee for Human Rights in North Korea, 2012); Andrei Lankov, *The Real North Korea: Life and Politics in the Failed Stalinist Utopia* (Oxford University Press, 2013); United Nations, *Report of the Commission of Inquiry on Human Rights in the Democratic People's Republic of Korea* (United Nations, 2014).

feature of Jang's very earliest memories dating back to the supposedly more prosperous 1970s. The descriptions she paints of
a society experiencing mass hunger and starvation are searing,
underlining not only the physical deprivation caused by the
North Korean famine and accompanying general economic
crisis, but the moral and social decay as well.

The "lean season" of late spring is a feature of many peasant
societies. And despite the gleaming monuments in Pyongyang,
North Korea was and remains a desperately poor country, particularly in the rural areas. But in North Korea, food deficits
are a result of politics as much as nature. Sunhwa continually
refers to the failure of work units and the public distribution
system to deliver rations to her and her family, and the struggles
her household and others endure to forage, barter and trade to
make ends meet.

The deprivation is not equally distributed, and Sunhwa talks
of the heretical rumours that those in Pyongyang were living
well at the expense of those in the countryside. Repeatedly, we
see evidence of unequal access to food on the basis of connections to the Party. And we see how Sunhwa's family—through
her mother's side—suffers further indignities because of the infamous *songbun* system of social classification. For every family
in North Korea, the Party keeps a file that contains information
deemed pertinent to its political loyalty. The paramount sins are
to have relatives who were collaborators with the Japanese, who
were capitalists or landlords or, perhaps worse still, who defected to the South during or immediately following the Korean
War. These transgressions, which are passed from generation to
generation, influence not only prospects for Party membership
(a continual theme in the book) but also job placement, educa-
tion, marriage and, ultimately, access to food. In effect, North
Korea is a caste society made up of the so-called core, wavering

and hostile classes, and a family's life chances are dictated by its social position.

In my work with Marcus Noland on the famine and food economy in North Korea, we also show how the survival strategies of families give rise to an underground economy. It is a theme that comes through clearly in this memoir. The official economy is purportedly state socialist, and we see the effects of state direction throughout the book as Sunhwa, her family and acquaintances are moved from work unit to work unit as the authorities demand. Yet we also see the nascent market economy that flourishes during the lean season—and particularly during the famine.

Also striking in this account is the ambivalence of the authorities toward this market economy. The state recognizes that, for human survival, citizens need to be able to trade and barter. Yet at the same time, the state fears the movement of citizens and continually subjects them to unpredictable controls. At the lowest level, police harass street vendors, extract bribes and exploit their power in the most brutal ways, particularly with respect to women, who are the dominant players in these unofficial markets.

Yet another important theme that emerges in the book is the significant role played by China in propping up the North Korean regime. I was particularly interested to read early in the narrative—in the 1970s—that Chinese traders had already made inroads into North Korea, but they gained an even larger foothold by the time of the famine, as the cross-border trade took off during the Arduous March. We see Sunhwa drawn into a common scheme at that time, taking available North Korean products like fish and dogs to China to get rice and other staples.

However, it is during her forays into China that Sunhwa experiences some of the most degrading experiences in her difficult life. While the North Koreans are shocked to see how much better life is outside their country, to the Chinese, people from Chosun are clearly second-class non-citizens. The central factor driving this mistreatment of North Koreans in China is the failure of the Chinese government to recognize them as refugees. Refugees are citizens leaving their country of origin who fear persecution on their return as a result of race, religion, nationality, political belief or membership in a particular social group, and it has been my position, and that of other analysts, that North Koreans leaving their country are almost by definition refugees. Since the Kim regime makes it a criminal offence to exit the country—in violation of widely accepted human rights norms and conventions—*all* North Koreans who leave live in fear of return and incarceration. The deplorable treatment that North Korean women experience—being trafficked and sold into slavery, separated from their children, abused by citizens and authorities—can all be traced to the failure of the Chinese government to abide by its commitments under the Refugee Convention. The Sunhwas of the world deserve the opportunity to apply for—and be granted—refugee status that will permit their humane treatment and resettlement.

Sadly, the account that Sunhwa relates in Part III about the infamous penal system of North Korea is all too common in refugee testimony; relatively rare are those who describe a clean getaway from North Korea without detention in China or return to North Korea. As in Sunhwa's case, some are incarcerated more than once.

The ideological commitments of the Kim regime provide the foundation for the utterly dehumanizing treatment, including pervasive sexual abuse and forced abortion, of the "traitors" in the prison system. In our surveys of refugees, we were surprised to find that the treatment in the "labour training" camps, like the ones to which Sunhwa was moved, were only marginally better than in the larger political concentration camps reserved for the returnees from China who revealed more political motives for departing. More than any other feature of the North Korean political system, the abuses of its prison system—including the grisly executions described in the book—rise most easily to the status of crimes against humanity, as the UN Commission of Inquiry on Human Rights in North Korea has also recently concluded in its defining report on the topic.

The indignities of the North Korean political system are not only revealed in the extremes of the prison camp scenes of the book. The effort of the regime to turn citizens against each another and to sow fear and suspicion across society as an instrument of control is a recurring theme throughout the memoir. The infamous Boweebu secret police are everywhere; it is impossible to know who can be trusted and who might be seeking advantage by revealing damning information to the authorities. Any attempts at organizing resistance are continually and self-consciously broken, not only through surveillance but by turning family against family, and even family member against family member.

I have read numerous refugee memoirs, but what never fails to amaze me is the strong theme of hope that runs through these remarkably courageous accounts. As the title of this book suggests, those who escape are often dreamers capable of imagining a different life for themselves and their children. Reading these stories of loss and deliverance should inspire all of us to work on behalf not only of the refugees—the tip of a much larger iceberg—but of those who are trapped behind as well. Just as North Koreans survive in part through acts of compassion and kindness, so the international community must continually bear witness to the indignities of the North Korean system. This memoir, and others like it, poses one of the central moral issues of our day: how to bring freedom to North Korea.

STEPHAN HAGGARD, PH.D., is the Lawrence and Sallye Krause Professor of Korea-Pacific Studies, director of the Korea-Pacific Program and Distinguished Professor of Political Science at UC San Diego School of International Relations and Pacific Studies. He is the author with Marcus Noland of *Famine in North Korea: Markets, Aid and Reform* (2007) and *Witness to Transformation: Refugee Insights into North Korea* (2011). They are also authors of the Witness to Transformation blog at http://blogs.piie.com/nk/.